# The Ghosts
## of
## Borley

# The Ghosts
## of
## Borley

Annals of the Haunted Rectory

## Peter Underwood
## and
## Paul Tabori

*DEDICATED*
*to the memory of*
*HARRY PRICE*
*the man who*
*put*
*Borley*
*on the map*

# Contents

# *Illustrations*

PLATES

MAPS AND PLANS

# Introduction

There is nothing left of Borley Rectory. A fire destroyed it on 27 February 1939; the burnt-out shell was demolished in 1944. And yet the argument about the phenomena, genuine and alleged, linked with the place, continues almost unabated. Three books, a book-length report published in the *Proceedings* of the Society for Psychical Research, innumerable articles, letters, public and private debates have been devoted to presenting or questioning the evidence, and several hundred trained investigators, journalists and laymen have spent an awesome number of man-hours describing this or that particular testimony. Borley has been used as a triumphant proof of survival after death and as a striking example of unscrupulous trickery. Because of the length of the period during which the phenomena were reported, and the complexity of the facts, it has become a classic case of protracted and often violent controversy such as occurs often enough in the world of the occult.

We feel the time has come to evaluate all the available evidence, to deal as objectively as possible with the charges and counter-charges, the passionate accusations and the equally fervent defences. One of us (PU) has spent many years gathering and analysing the vast material; the other (PT) has been Harry Price's literary executor for the past quarter of a century. Both of us have made extensive research into the Borley case over a long period. It is only fair that we should declare our bias here and now: for reasons that we hope to make apparent we believe that at least some of the phenomena were genuine and for equally valid reasons we must reject the indictment brought against the author of *The Most Haunted House in England* and *The End of Borley Rectory*.

Much of the war over Borley originated in the personalities and attitudes of the principal characters. Harry Price, who died in March 1948, though he was a member and occasionally the founder of a number of research organisations, was basically a lone wolf. He was never comfortable working within the disciplines of the Society for Psychical Research; a maverick, quick-tempered, self-assertive, vain and never averse to publicity, he made enemies easily and did not suffer fools gladly. His career and his character are expounded in the biography one of us (PT) wrote, and we have no intention of dealing with these aspects except in so far as they are pertinent to the Borley story. But it must be mentioned here that any accusations brought against Price—accusations of bad faith, duplicity and downright deception—did not really surface until nine months after his death, and the SPR critical survey of the Borley hauntings was published eight years later.

A former president of the Society for Psychical Research stated that this body was concerned with investigation and not matters of belief. That is fair enough, though the fact that X has not had any occult experiences is hardly sufficient justification for denying that Y or Z might have had them. Doubt can be a trait of character, a quality imprinted upon the brain—sometimes so powerful that it cannot be overcome by the most tangible evidence. And of course, wounds which Thomases can touch are rare enough. Others, again, may be too eager and too ready to believe—and refuse to give up their faith in the face of the most damning proof. Finally, there are people who wish to reserve judgement. By and large the SPR has always refused to make allowances for the differences between these three approaches. Its declared object has been to investigate 'without prejudice or prepossession'. This is an attitude that deserves respect but it is not the only possible one. The human element is paramount in psychical phenomena and this element is ignored at the investigator's peril. Here, as in the physical sciences, Heisenberg's principle according to which the very act of observation changes and influences the observed object is clearly applicable. To deny this means the danger of one-sidedness and the rejection of a whole range of possibilities and even probabilities.

The publication of *The Haunting of Borley Rectory* by Dr E. J. Dingwall, Mrs K. M. Goldney and Mr T. H. Hall (it appeared simultaneously in the *Proceedings* of the SPR and as a book from Duckworth & Co.) was intended to establish Price's guilt and to destroy, once and for all, the 'Borley Legend'. It was the case for the prosecution with no allowance for the defence or for any independent judgement. We are neither questioning the good faith of its authors (though some of them have been accused of excessive severity and total scepticism) nor have we any intention of answering their charges point by point. A member of the SPR, Robert J. Hastings, has undertaken this onerous task. It is certainly a proof of the Society's fair-mindedness that in 1965 it authorised re-examination of the Borley files and made a grant in aid of expenses. The Hastings report was published in March 1969 and was widely reviewed and commented on. Some said that it vindicated Harry Price completely; others (especially the authors of the 1956 publication) denied this. The argument still continues and if we deal with it, we hope we do so in a non-partisan and civilised spirit. In the final analysis it is for the reader to make up his mind—or, if he feels qualified, to take up any further points for himself.

Our own book presents a chronological account of the Borley story, though we have, in each case, tried to follow our principal characters or the principal events to their logical conclusion even if this meant moving ahead of time. Thus, dealing with the incumbencies of the various rectors, we have traced their subsequent careers and, wherever this was necessary, the careers of their families. We have introduced everywhere the latest evidence, the most up-to-date statements. We hope that we have avoided excessive detail without skimping the important and telling facts. If we have not always succeeded in writing *sine ira et studio,* at least we have tried to make it clear where and in what way our views differ from those of others.

We believe that the Borley hauntings represent one of the most interesting, most cohesive and varied chapters in the history of psychical research and that they contain, as if in a microcosm, the whole range of psychic phenomena. It is our hope that the reader will share this belief when he has finished our work.

We acknowledge our indebtedness to the many correspondents who have reported apparently paranormal activity at Borley over the years; to people like James Turner, the Bull family, the Hennings and all the others who had first-hand knowledge of Borley and its mysteries. We are especially grateful to Alan Roper for much original research in respect of some of the chief actors in the Borley drama.

We also wish to thank the individuals and organisations acknowledged on pp9–10 for permission to reproduce photographs, maps and plans.

London
June 1973

Peter Underwood
Paul Tabori

# 1
# *Borley and the Bulls*

Borley Rectory, two-and-a-half miles from Sudbury, Suffolk, stood on the north bank of the river Stour where it divides the counties of Suffolk and Essex. Built on the Essex side, it served a parish that in 1931 contained a mere 121 people. The nearest stations were at Sudbury and Long Melford, about sixty miles from London on the former London and North-Eastern Railway.

There is some evidence that the Rectory, completed in 1863, stood on the site of a much earlier building. Borley church, just across the road, was erected in the twelfth century.

When he was inducted to the living of Borley in 1862, the Reverend Henry Dawson Ellis Bull MA was living at Borley Place, a fine sixteenth-century house which practically adjoins the church. Immediately he set to building a new rectory, an L-shaped building, and there he lived for the rest of his life. As his family increased (he fathered at least fourteen children) he kept adding to his home and by 1892 it had grown into an irregular, sprawling conglomeration which almost enclosed an open courtyard in the centre. Two large bay-windows, a glass-roofed verandah and a number of french windows faced south-east where a large lawn and gardens were laid out, narrowing to a point, dotted with copper-beech, cedars of Lebanon and elm trees. The long path that skirted the lawn on the south side later became known as the 'Nun's Walk'. About a hundred yards from the house a large, octagonal pavilion faced the Nun's Walk; at the far end of the property, some two hundred yards from the house, there was a small mock-Gothic summer-house. Between the two there was a former cats' cemetery with headboards marking the graves of long-vanished Gems, Rollos and Sandies. A tiny stream that emptied into a pond cut the garden almost into two. Part of the garden was believed to have been the burial place of some of the victims of the Great Plague of 1664-5. Persistent rumours spoke of a network of underground tunnels; one was supposed to run between an old nunnery at Bures and Borley (a distance of seven miles!) and to have been used by at least one pair of lovers for their trysts. Their tragic story became part of the Borley legend.

The Rectory's front door and porch were set facing the road. A broad drive bordered by a high holly hedge and trees separated the road from the house. The porch had a separate door. In addition to the french windows of the library and the front door, there were also back doors which led from the courtyard into the scullery and kitchen passage; another small door gave access from the garden to the main hall. Most of the windows had shutters; those in the domestic quarters were heavily barred. One, facing the carriage drive, was bricked up. There were nine rooms and the large hall on the ground floor, with many cupboards, a store closet and cellars. There was no gas, electricity or main water supply. The marble mantelpiece in the dining-room was decorated with the busts of two monks; it was claimed to have been exhibited at the 1851 Great Exhibition. The solidly built cellars could be reached by a staircase from the kitchen passage and extended under the main hall, the major part of the library and a corner of the dining-room, in addition to the passage itself. They were divided by partition walls. A shallow well, its opening in the courtyard, reached into the portion of the cellars that lay under the kitchen passage. There is little doubt that parts of the cellars belonged to an earlier building;

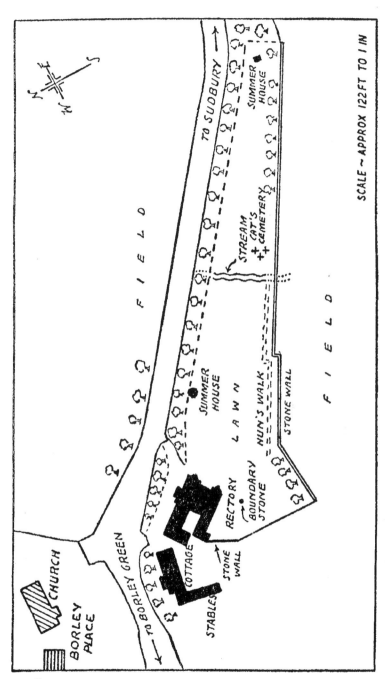

Map of Borley Rectory; the grounds comprised nearly three and three-quarter acres

B

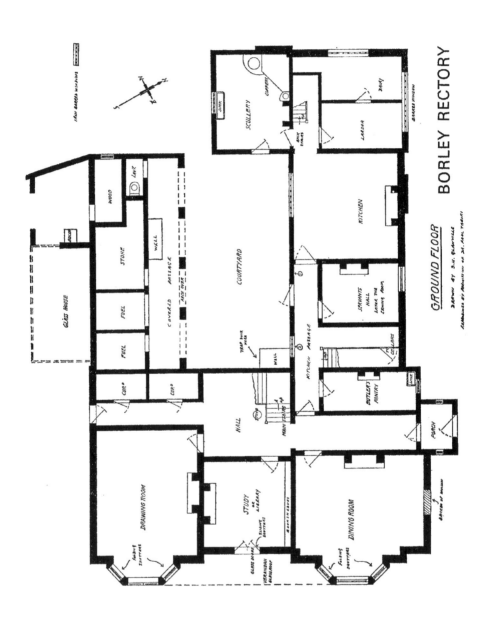

BORLEY RECTORY

GROUND FLOOR

DRAWN BY J. H. GLANVILLE

ASSEMBLED BY MEASURING or BY REAL TESTS

a fact established by excavation in 1955 (see Chapter 5). Entry to the Rectory could also have been through the cellar opening in the courtyard.

From the ground floor three staircases led to the first floor which had fourteen rooms, including a large lavatory, a capacious bathroom and the so-called 'chapel'. On either side of the Blue Room (one of the principal bedrooms) there were two arches over the landing. Between the lavatory and the bathroom, stairs led to the attics. Here were the water cistern and the anchor-board of the bell-levers and bells that hung in the kitchen passage.

Close to the Rectory stood an unattached building that had been the stables with living accommodation in the upper part. This building, which escaped the 1939 fire, was subsequently converted into a cottage and has been the home of the successive owners of the Rectory site.

Both the site and the buildings were the centre of many legends of haunts and ghostly happenings. A nun, a groom or monk, a coach-and-horses and various other apparitions have all been reported at one time or another at Borley. The various versions and local rumours all centred on the assumption that there was once a monastery on or near the Rectory site and that a groom or lay brother fell in love with a beautiful young novice from a nearby nunnery. The lovers would meet in the nearby woods. At length they eloped in a black coach drawn by a pair of bay horses and driven by another lay brother. They were soon missed, however, and their superiors set out in pursuit. The fleeing couple were caught; the would-be bridegroom was hanged, the girl bricked up alive.

It is a romantic tale, not without parallels; a pity that no evidence has ever been discovered of a monastery existing at Borley. Nor has any trace been found of a nunnery at nearby Bures. No record exists of any nuns ever being walled up alive in Britain, though some cases of this punishment have

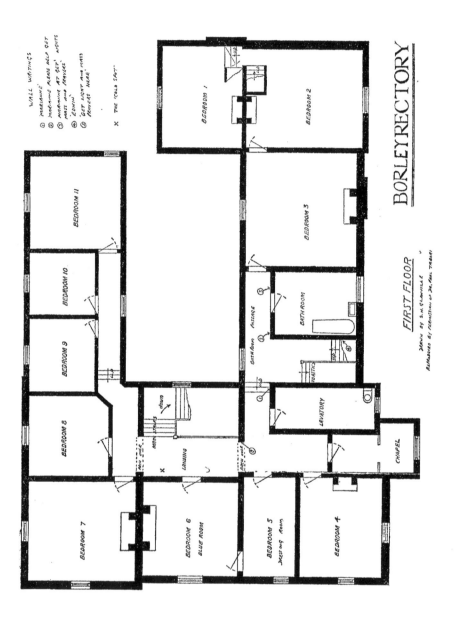

BORLEY RECTORY

FIRST FLOOR

DRAWN BY S.H. GLANVILLE
REARRANGED BY REPRODUCTION BY DR. PAUL TABORI

WALL WRITINGS

① MARIANNE
② MARIANNE PLEASE HELP GET
③ MARIANNE AT GET KAYTE'S
   MASS AND PRAYERS
④ EDWIN
⑤ GET LIGHT AND MASS
   PRAYERS HERE

X THE "COLD SPOT"

BEDROOM 1
BEDROOM 2
BEDROOM 3
BEDROOM 11
BEDROOM 10
BEDROOM 9
BEDROOM 8
BEDROOM 7
BEDROOM 6
BLUE ROOM
BEDROOM 5
SLEEPING ROOM
BEDROOM 4
BATHROOM
PASSAGE
BATHROOM
LAVATORY
CHAPEL
LANDING
MAIN STAIRS
down

been known on the Continent.

We have, however, clear enough evidence that the Bull family lived in and around Borley for centuries. Anne Boleyn, Henry VIII's unhappy queen (whose name was also spelled Bullen) had a house at nearby Bulmer. She, her brother and her alleged lovers were all beheaded; many partisans of Catherine of Aragon, her predecessor, regarded her family as evil and they were much hated at the time. There have been suggestions that the Boleyns or Bullens (those who survived) adopted a slightly different name and that the Bulls of Borley were their descendants—though here again genealogical data are missing or are vague.

Certainly, the Reverend Henry D. E. Bull and his wife knew about the legend of the ghostly nun. They were even. said to have built the large pavilion in the garden for the express purpose of watching for her appearances. During their lifetime the walk bordering the lawn became known as the 'Nun's Walk'.

The first rector and his wife both died at the Rectory and are buried in the churchyard there. With the Reverend Henry Bull's passing away in 1892 thirty years' incumbency came to an end. He was succeeded by his son, the Reverend 'Harry' Foyster Bull, who held the living until his death in 1927, that is, for thirty-five years. In 1911 he married a widow who had a daughter by her previous marriage. Mrs Harry Bull died at Hastings in 1955.

At the time of his marriage Harry Bull lived at Borley Place (where he was born); when his mother died in 1914, he and his wife stayed on for another six years, until 1920, when they moved into the Rectory. At the same time his sisters, who had lived there, moved out. It was in the Blue Room that Harry Bull died on 9 June 1927 and he, too, is buried in Borley churchyard.

During the lifetime of the Reverend H. D. E. Bull many incidents of a curious and allegedly paranormal nature were recorded. As related by three of his daughters, the Misses Ethel, Freda and Mabel Bull (who gave full accounts to Harry Price and Sidney H. Glanville, one of Price's chief associates in the Borley investigation), footsteps followed by taps were frequently heard at night; the bells rang without any explanation—once all twenty of them pealed out simultaneously for no apparent reason. One night one of the Bull girls was awakened by something or someone invisible slapping her face. At least once, Miss Ethel Bull awoke suddenly to find the dark figure of an old man wearing a tall hat standing beside her bed. Miss Ethel told Peter Underwood of this encounter with the 'tall, dark man' in the Rectory. She saw him quite distinctly, standing beside her bed dressed in dark clothes. On one or two other occasions she 'felt sure someone was sitting on her bed'—though no one was visible. Mrs E. Byford, a nursemaid who spent a short time at the Rectory in 1886, reported footsteps she could not explain and the whole atmosphere of the place made her so nervous that she left.

Mr P. Shaw Jeffrey MA, a former headmaster of Colchester Royal Grammar School, visited the Rectory in 1885 or 1886 and claimed to have seen the famous 'Nun' several times. By the time he told his story he was of great age and hesitant about possible dates but he was quite emphatic that he had visited Borley during the long vacations (he was a fellow-student of Harry Bull at Oxford) and that not only had he caught several glimpses of the 'Nun' but that his friend Harry told him of his own experiences of the same nature. In 1950 he was asked for further help in exploring those distant days, but he said, fairly enough: 'I am afraid I shall be of no use to you. I am eighty-eight in a few days' time; my memory is quite untrustworthy and the events at Borley . . . so remote that they now seem quite unreal and I should not be prepared to swear to them.' Yet Mr Jeffrey (who died in 1952) did not deny or retract or even modify any of his previous evidence—

given in 1942, when he was much younger.

In February 1954 the 86-year-old brother of the Reverend L. A. Foyster (who was one of the later incumbents of Borley Rectory) showed Peter Underwood a photograph of the late Mrs H. D. E. Bull and spoke of at least one occasion when the lady saw the 'Nun' herself. She told her husband, who recalled that it was the reputed anniversary of the Nun's 'regular appearance'. Mr Foyster was emphatic in stating that the Reverend H. D. E. Bull knew all about the famous 'Nun' and the dates on which she was supposed to appear. Miss Ethel Bull herself, in a letter written on 22 September 1954, said she 'quite expects' that her parents 'knew about the nun but the children were never told'. She and her sisters had obviously become quite accustomed to the curious happenings and took little notice of them. Conceivably, had her brother Harry or anyone else told her of having seen an apparition or of hearing something apparently inexplicable, it would have made no great impression on her memory. This may explain the fact that in 1950 she replied to an enquiry by saying that she did not recall hearing of the 'nun-like figure' being seen before 1900.

During the thirty-five years of Harry Bull's incumbency the story of the haunting grew and spread. 'Old Harry' was described by a regular army officer who was frequently at the Rectory during these years and often played tennis with him as 'one of the most normal men one could meet'. But he was quite definitely interested in allegedly paranormal phenomena. He would spend hours, particularly between 10 pm and 3 am in the summer-house facing the Nun's Walk. A doctor friend of Harry Bull told one of us (PU) that 'he could hail a spectre as easily as most people can hail a friend'. His wife, like the servants at that time, was not particularly interested in the ghosts and just appeared to take the hauntings, including the 'existence' of the 'Nun', for granted.

Harry Bull was a typical squire-parson, a lovable and easy-going man with a great sense of humour; he used to tear across to the church for matins and be back in nine-and-a-half minutes. 'Oh! very puff!' he would exclaim. 'Never missed a word and broke my own record!'

Harry Bull made no secret of his varied psychical experiences; he told dozens of people about seeing the ghostly nun and hearing the phantom coach-and-horses. He also spoke of other 'psychic experiences' at Felix Bull's rectory at Pentlow and other places.

At the very beginning of Harry Bull's incumbency, soon after his father's death, there was a recurrent phenomenon at Borley: someone was heard entering the back door. Although this was promptly and repeatedly investigated, no explanation was forthcoming.

In 1900, when Harry Bull had been at Borley Rectory for eight years, three of his sisters were returning one afternoon from a garden party. It was July. As they entered by the lower gate, the Nun's Walk was clearly visible in front of them. Almost immediately, they glimpsed a dark female figure, gliding with bowed head in the direction of the little stream. The sisters were terrified; two of them stopped by the large summer-house and watched while the other ran into the house and fetched another sister who also saw the figure but refused to believe that there was anything strange about the shape; she moved forward to intercept it, whereupon the apparition stopped, turned its face towards the Rectory and then vanished.

It was Miss Ethel Bull who told us some years ago that the accounts which Harry Price gave in his book of this now famous and much-debated incident were not entirely accurate. She and her sisters saw the figure in rather poor light at a distance of perhaps a hundred yards; no features were distinguishable and no white or light colouring was noticeable. On the other hand, all four sisters were convinced that they had seen a figure whose presence was inexplicable—and who disappeared tracelessly. All four ladies lived past the biblical span and told identical, consistent stories of the experience for over fifty years. We spent some time on a number of occasions in the company of the surviving members of the Bull family at their charming home, Chilton Lodge, Great Cornard; and these meetings made it difficult to dismiss the 1900 'incident' as mere hallucination or, even less, as an invention. Less than four months after the 28 July 1900 appearance, Miss Ethel Bull and the Rectory cook saw the same figure leaning over a gate. A cousin, while staying in the house, is also reported to have seen it. And of course, there is the earlier testimony of Mr Jeffrey which we have already quoted. Collective hallucination? Some hypnotic influence? The options are varied but by no means unlimited.

The Reverend Harry Bull also had a number of curious experiences. Once he was in the garden with his retriever when the dog suddenly started to howl and cowered in fright. When the Rector looked in the apparent direction of the dog's terrified gaze, he saw the legs of a figure; the rest was hidden by the branches of heavily-laden fruit bushes. The legs moved and when they were clear of the bushes, the figure of a headless man emerged. Harry Bull offered no explanation (the story was repeated by Miss Ethel Bull to Harry Price), nor was any sought.

On another occasion Harry Bull told of seeing a 'little old man, standing with his arms pointing, one up and one down, in the middle of the lawn'. His features, according to Bull, were identical with those of a former gardener; he vanished when the Rector approached. Harry Bull was said to have seen the phantom coach drawn by two horses and driven by a headless coachman several times. (The lack of a head is, of course, a recurrent *motif* in many ghost stories, perhaps to add to the horror of such an apparition.) As he watched, the whole ghostly group disappeared. One night, as he was about to enter the Rectory gate, he heard a great clatter of hooves and the rumbling of heavy wheels in the roadway. As he stepped to one side, he heard the sounds pass along the road but there was nothing visible to account for them.

Among several others, Harry Bull discussed these curious experiences with the Reverend Harry Carpenter quite freely. He described in detail the appearance in the conservatory of an unidentified man who vanished. He talked about the 'Nun' to the Reverend W. G. Stote, to Sir George and Lady White-house, to Mr J. Harley of Cavendish and the Reverend Clive Luget of Middleton. One of the accounts he gave to Mr Farrance, a local parishioner, was quite elaborate: according to it the 'Nun' had followed him from the churchyard down the path to the Rectory front door. (This version was passed on by Mr Farrance's son to the Reverend A. C. Henning, another incumbent at Borley, who related it to Harry Price. in 1943.)

Mr Harley, whom Peter Underwood visited at his home in Cavendish in September 1952, provided many incidents about life at the Rectory in the days of the Reverend Harry Bull. Once when Mr Harley was spending the night at Borley, a loud peal of bells awakened him and Harry Bull appeared, wearing his favourite plum-coloured dressing-gown, carrying a candle. He was greatly upset about the ringing of the bells and thought that it might foretell some misfortune for the family or for himself in particular. On another occasion, in the presence of Mr Harley, Harry Bull ('a puckish, lovable man', as his friend described him) said that if after his death he was dissatisfied with his successor, he would try to make his displeasure felt in some unusual way—'such as throwing moth-balls about!' Moth-balls were inexplicably thrown, on at least one occasion, inside the Rectory.

'She was extraordinarily active last night,' Harry Bull would sometimes tell Mr Harley, speaking of the 'Nun'. 'I can usually tell.' Harley himself often felt as if he were being watched and followed in the Rectory; not by anyone hostile but by someone who took rather more than a cursory interest in his movements. In an article published in the *East Anglian Daily Times* on 15 March 1956 he described it as 'a curious sensation impossible to explain but not in the least frightening'.

At this period there seemed to have been a hopeless feeling at the Rectory—as if whatever one did, things would never come out right at the end; it must have been a profound influence to affect a boy of fifteen—Mr Harley's age at the time.

Critics of the Borley hauntings have suggested that the alleged apparitions seen by the Reverend Harry Bull were 'illusions or perhaps hallucinations for which no explanation other than a morbid imagination and evident interest in the supernormal is necessary'. In addition the sceptics stated that the 'Nun' was not claimed to have been seen by anyone since the Bull incumbency, with the exception of three 'rather dubious experiences'. In actual fact there have been over a dozen reports of an unexplained nun-like figure in the vicinity of the Rectory (up to 1946), including some occasions when the figure was seen by two or more people at the same time. There is ample evidence that the ghost nun has been seen many times in the last twenty-odd years, according to various statements.

Between 1924 and 1927 Mrs W. Newman was employed as a cook and lived at the Rectory. Her bedroom had two doors: one leading to the bathroom passage, the other to Room 2, which she called the 'Pear Room' as it was often used for storing pears and other fruit. Mrs Newman would carefully lock both doors of her room each night before retiring to bed and leave the keys inside the locks. Yet morning after morning she would find the door leading to the Pear Room unlocked and the door wide open. Finally, after locking the Pear Room door, she removed the key—which stopped the 'interference'. The only other access to Mrs Newman's room was a window overlooking the courtyard, many feet below. This window remained untouched, though it was often closed when the Pear Room door mysteriously opened during the night. (This is just one piece of evidence which was not dealt with in the critical SPR report, and its authors did not question Mrs Newman, among many other witnesses.)

Walter Bull (one of H. D. E. Bull's sons), who was described as 'utterly unbelieving', once stated that he heard *on at least fifty occasions* footsteps following him down the lane leading to the Rectory. Walter Bull has been quoted as saying that while the Bulls lived there, 'nothing abnormal ever happened in the Rectory'. Of course, his own experiences of the mysterious footsteps all took place outside. Gerald Bull, another brother, told Canon Lawton that he had never seen anything of an abnormal nature during all the years he spent at Borley; being entirely sceptical, he held the view that the 'Nun' was a 'figment of feminine imagination'. The Misses Bull, it seems, were mildly proud of the tradition of the family ghost, publicly telling the tale of the 'phantom in the garden' —but they never spoke to Canon Lawton (who knew the Bulls very well indeed) with any degree of seriousness about the matter. Thus there was certainly considerable division within the one family whose association with the Rectory was the longest and most extensive. As happens often enough in hauntings, the individuals changed their opinions and varied their statements in the course of the years. Yet whether they did or did not believe in the 'Nun', the phantom coaches and other spectacular apparitions, practically everyone who lived there and scores of visitors asserted that the place *was* haunted; and the hauntings, according to the various testimonies, began soon after the Rectory was built and continued for over seventy years. And it seems to have been during the Bulls' occupancy that it acquired the name of 'the most haunted house in England'.

# 2
# *The Smiths Come and Go*

When Harry Bull died in June 1927, the reputation of Borley Rectory was sufficiently sinister to make difficult the finding of a successor. It was not until sixteen months later, in October 1928, that the Reverend G. Eric Smith was inducted to the living. And the Smiths stayed a mere nine months.

Yet the Smiths' brief tenancy was an important turning-point in the psychic history of Borley. Though they never really settled down—before very long they found a number of curious things happening that made Mrs Smith particularly nervous and frightened, while her husband was considerably puzzled—it was this third incumbent who wrote to a national paper about the Borley events. In turn, it was the *Daily Mirror* that first sent down a reporter, V. C. Wall, to look into the matter, and at the same time the paper also got in touch with Harry Price. The first press report on the Borley phenomena was published on 10 June 1929. Two days later Price visited the Rectory, accompanied by Miss Lucy Kaye (later Mrs Meeker), his secretary.

During that first visit, which marked the beginning of Price's investigation, he talked to a number of people, taking statements from all of them without committing himself in any way to belief or scepticism.

He talked to the Reverend G. Eric Smith and his wife, whom he described as 'intelligent, much travelled and sceptical people who were puzzled by what was happening and what had been reported to have happened at the Rectory'. He saw Miss Ethel Bull who was residing at Great Cornard. He spoke to Miss Mary Pearson, a maid at the Rectory, and to Mr and Mrs Edward Cooper who had lived at the cottage adjoining the Rectory from 1916 until 1920. (Mr Cooper had been employed by the Bull family for many years.)

All these people—with the important exception of Mrs Smith—remained consistent in their accounts, which they repeated to various investigators during the years to come.

The Smiths spoke of 'sibilant whisperings' heard several times by the Rector as he passed under the archway on the landing. Once he thought he caught the words: 'Don't, Carlos, don't!' The mysterious bell-ringing, experienced by the Bulls, also plagued the Smiths—and they, too, failed to establish any human agency that could have been responsible for it. Slow and deliberate footsteps paced the passages and upper rooms. Two maidservants successively employed by the Smiths saw 'apparitions'. The traditional figure of the 'Nun' was reported passing along her 'Walk' and a similar figure was seen to disappear at the bottom of the garden. An upper window appeared to light up inexplicably—and Mrs Smith pointed this out to various neighbours. A shadowy shape was seen leaning over one of the drive gates; when it was investigated, there was nothing to account for it. One of the maids claimed that she saw the traditional coach-and-horses; she said she saw it on the lawn before it disappeared into the hedge bordering the road. Curious noises were heard, more frequently in the winter months than in the summer. Keys unaccountably shot out of locks. A vase from an upstairs window was found smashed to pieces at the foot of the main stairs. (Apart from telling Harry Price about all this, the Smiths also referred to many of these 'inexplicable' happenings in letters to another distinguished psychic investigator, Lord Charles Hope, who first visited the Rectory on 5 July 1929, together with Price and Miss Kaye.)

On the occasion of Price's first visit two of the Misses Bull had come to Borley from their home at Great Cornard. It was decided to hold a séance in the Blue Room. The improvised circle was made up of the Smiths, the Misses Bull, Price, Miss Kaye and Mr Wall. The séance began at 1am. Price opened the proceedings by calling upon any entity that might be present 'to make itself known'. After he had repeated this request several times, taps were heard, emanating apparently from the wooden back of a solid mahogany mirror standing on a dressing-table. Chairs were drawn up around this table and, following a succession of short, sharp raps, a code was evolved and answers were obtained to direct questions. By this means it seemed to be established that the 'communicator' was none other than Harry Bull. He 'accepted responsibility' for the footsteps in the house but insisted that he did not wish to worry or annoy anyone, merely to attract attention. He agreed that if a medium were present more information could be obtained. Next the Misses Bull, the Rector and Mrs Smith asked questions 'on personal matters' for about an hour. Later Miss Ethel Bull told Peter Underwood that she was utterly convinced that 'no living person could have known the answers given to some of her questions that night'.

At about two o'clock the group seated around the dressing-table were startled by a noise—a new cake of soap had apparently jumped out of its dish and on to the floor. This small incident later led to Price being accused of trickery. We questioned Miss Ethel Bull about it and she replied (in a letter dated 22 September 1954): 'I honestly don't think Harry Price tried any tricks.' Mr Wall, the *Daily Mirror* reporter, described the episode in his article which appeared two days after the visit to Borley:

> From one o'clock until nearly four o'clock this morning all of us, including the Rector and his wife, actually questioned the spirit or whatever it was and received at times the most emphatic

answers. A cake of soap on the washstand was lifted and thrown
heavily on to a china jug standing on the floor with such force
that the soap was deeply marked. All of us were at the other
side of the room when this happened.

Mr and Mrs Smith found that the mirror used at this
séance continued to be 'alive' after they left Borley. It produced raps that were clearly marked and in series. The Smiths
ignored them. As late at 14 November 1937 Mrs Smith suggested to Mr Glanville, Price's associate, that it would be a
good idea to 'take the mirror that "tapped" to Borley in order
to promote demonstrations'.

Much of the confusion and mystery around this first séance
arose out of the later ambivalent attitude of Mrs Mabel
Smith. When Price described this visit, he spoke of 'the excellent supper that the hospitable Mrs Smith had prepared'
and of an undisturbed night in the Blue Room 'in the cosy
bed Mrs Smith had prepared for me'. Some sixteen years later,
however, the same 'hospitable' lady stated that Price was 'very
unwelcome and suspected of all kinds of trickery'. Her change
of mind seems to have occurred some time after 1937, for in
that year her husband wrote to Sidney H. Glanville, following
the latter's suggestion that Price should join a combined visit
to Borley. The Reverend Smith said: 'It would indeed be a
great pleasure to renew the fellowship of sight and hand with
Mr Price, so do please tell him to come'.

Mrs Smith later declared that the séance in the Blue Room
was stopped by her husband who refused to have it continued
when 'indiscreet' questions were asked and answers given. She
added, however, that little lights or sparks appeared at the
séance. Once, when Price was in a room with her, small
pebbles whizzed past them. She remarked, somewhat illogi-
cally, that 'she could not help thinking that perhaps he had
something to do with them'. Another time there was a guest
sitting next to Price at dinner in the Rectory who remarked

that all these 'apparent mysteries' could be manufactured by a clever man. Before very long the water in her glass turned to ink. At least, that is what Mrs Smith reported in 1949, a considerable time after the 'event'. This was the first time anyone heard about this extraordinary 'transformation scene'. In a letter she wrote to Mr Glanville (dated 29 November 1937) Mrs Smith referred to the shutters in the library 'making peculiar noises'. These she and her husband put down to the wind—'until that night when they were pulled together, seemingly by no one . . .'

Edward Cooper, the former gardener and groom of the Bull family, also gave some facts to Harry Price. For over three years, he told the London visitor, when he and his wife were in bed at the Rectory cottage they were disturbed most nights by 'the sounds of pattering feet as of a large dog'; the sounds appeared to come from the adjoining living-room. The Coopers never found any explanation for these noises— but one night they also heard a loud crash as though all the china on the kitchen dresser had been hurled to the floor. Nothing, in fact, was disturbed, but from then on they never heard the padding noise again.

One night in 1919, soon after dawn, the Coopers saw what appeared to be a 'black shape' running round their bedroom. Before they could do anything, it vanished. Looking out of his bedroom window one bright moonlit night, Mr Cooper happened to see the traditional coach. He had, as we mentioned before, also seen the 'Nun', or at least 'a black shape resembling a hooded figure', crossing the courtyard.

The Coopers left Borley in March 1920 and lived for the rest of their lives at nearby Sudbury. They never had any further psychic experiences.

Around the middle of 1929, a number of small objects 'appeared' inside the Rectory—seemingly as a result of poltergeist activity. They included a number of keys, pebbles and an eight-sided brass medal or medallion, bearing on the face the head of St Ignatius and on the reverse the word *ROMA*, beneath a design incorporating two human figures. Other medals that appeared equally inexplicably at Borley have been described as a 'small gilt medallion, such as are presented to Roman Catholic children on their confirmation', and a medal or badge 'dated *AN VIII* (*AD* 1799) issued in Paris after the French Revolution'. We still do not know where these medals came from. When Price's work at Borley was attacked, he was charged with having planted them. Apart from the fact that Price never collected foreign medals or coins, he must have been a remarkable clairvoyant to foresee that, eleven years after these medallions were found, Canon Phythian-Adams would produce a theory as to the Borley hauntings—involving a French nun or novice. Certainly, in 1929, Price had no inkling of any such concept being put forward—and thus to 'plant' anything that referred to Roman Catholicism or the eighteenth century would have been somewhat pointless.

A good deal of the charges against Price came out of the curious attitude of Mrs Smith. She communicated her experiences (hearing bells, 'voices', seeing shadowy figures and strange lights and repeatedly finding keys and other objects moved) to many people, indicating that, at least in some instances, she believed them to be of supernormal origin. Later (much later) she would provide different versions, completely at variance with her own earlier accounts and with those of others.

In 1949, twenty years after their brief stay at Borley, Mrs Smith gave an interview to Mrs K. M. Goldney. Mrs Goldney reported that she found her a middle-aged, practical, sensible woman who told her tale consistently and without any contradictions, a woman with a firm belief in an afterlife and open-minded as to the possibility of spirit communication. Yet she was emphatic in her assertion that 99 per cent if not 100 per cent of the Borley phenomena were 'normally produced'. She added that although she and her husband knew nothing of the supposed haunting when they went to Borley, they heard plenty about it soon after they arrived. There was plenty of gossip and rumours were flying; the local people even refused to come to the Rectory for parish meetings. She herself, as she put it in 1949, had no reason to think that Borley Rectory was haunted in 1929 and nothing occurred that she did not consider explicable. She admitted that her husband once heard a voice that sounded like: 'Don't, Carlos, don't!' and that he could not trace the source. But she felt that the villagers 'played tricks' and windows and doors were sometimes found open in ways that neither she nor her husband could explain.

She went on to say that she felt Price and her husband may have met in the afterlife. She believed that Price must have now realised 'the harm he did by adding to rumours and getting so much publicity for silly tales' and that the psychic researcher 'must now want it all to stop'. By helping to bring this about, she thought, she could bring him rest.

Thus, in 1949, Mrs Smith interpreted the Borley phenomena in terms of village gossip, the traditional legend, rats and mice, practical jokes and light-hearted stories invented by her maid. The facts, she added, were distorted and exaggerated by Price for the purposes of publicity; she even alleged that Price produced some of the 'effects' by deliberate trickery.

There does seem to be a serious discrepancy between Mrs Smith's statements at the time when she found the events definitely frightening and her attitude twenty years later. One explanation could be that she wished to remain on good terms with Price because of the latter's possible help with the publication of a manuscript Mrs Smith had written. In reply to persistent questioning by Mrs Goldney, she agreed she 'felt certain at the time that Borley Rectory was *not* haunted'. She said she did not know what to think when an expert like Harry Price arrived and unexplained phenomena occurred in his presence. She concluded the interview: 'Borley has strange memories, very mixed, and if it were not that I feel something impelling me to try and stop all the dangerous talk and publicity round the place, I do not think I should reopen this closed book of the past . . . I candidly do not think Eric ever believed that the place was haunted . . . '

Of course, Mrs Smith did not succeed in stopping the 'dangerous talk and publicity' connected with the place she had left two decades earlier. As for her motives, these are necessarily a matter of conjecture. Certainly her apparent change of mind is a good illustration of the psychological factors that must be taken into consideration whenever any testimony is recorded and evaluated. States of mind vary, contradictory beliefs can be entertained even within short periods. Unwelcome facts and unpleasant memories are suppressed, pushed into the subconscious—something psychoanalysis has explored and utilised to a large extent.

Obviously, Mrs Smith *wanted* to believe in 1949 that the disturbances had a 'perfectly normal explanation'. She was by no means an anti-spiritualist, accepting the possibility of spirit communication and, in addition, had a strong conviction that she possessed, all her life, 'almost a sixth sense of intuition and perception'. At the same time she felt that Price, 'perhaps suffering in the Beyond for all his mistakes and wrong-doings on earth, would welcome any action taken to arrest the mischief he had done and the untrue picture of Borley Rectory he fostered'. It is, of course, an interesting question whether such a belief was more or less rational than the acceptance of the paranormal nature of the Borley phenomena!

Mrs Smith much dreaded further publicity—yet at the time of Price's investigation she had actually written a novel incorporating them. This was called *Murder at the Parsonage* and she had tried to enlist Price's help in getting it published. The attempt failed—which may have left some resentment in

the would-be authoress. Her statements, made some twenty
years after her stay at the Rectory, were obvious ammunition
for the critics and opponents of Price's work—even though
they were at complete variance with the story she and her
husband had told to a number of people in 1929. The impression she made on various people added to this dichotomy.
(Borley was discussed in 1949 over lunch at Woburn Place by
Peter Underwood, Mrs. Goldney and the late Mr W. H. Salter,
then Secretary of the Society for Psychical Research; later
Peter Underwood met Mrs Smith.)

On 28 September 1945, the *Church Times* devoted its edi-
torial column to a review of Harry Price's *Poltergeist Over
England* which contained a long chapter on the Borley Rectory haunt. It was by no means hostile. In the next issue the
weekly carried a letter from the Reverend C. Sinclair, Rector
of Chale, in which he described experiences he and his wife
had at Chale Rectory soon after their arrival in 1940. '. . . persons who in the palmier days of the living had been maids in
the Rectory', Mr Sinclair wrote, claimed that strange things
happened—'including the driving into the yard at midnight
of a carriage and pair, which was said to have been heard,
but not seen, on many occasions.' The Sinclairs were all agog
on arrival for the manifestations, nor were they to be disappointed; they heard jingling as of harness, creaks, clangings,
grinding and jarring sounds and a 'rather stagey horses-hooves
noise' of a somewhat 'coconutty' quality. Other disturbances
included preserves and objects being knocked off shelves,
stealthy footsteps on landings, 'cold spots' and mysterious
'vigils' of the cat and dog outside closed doors of empty rooms.
Even pencil-scribbling was discovered, but this was established as being the work of a sub-tenant's child. One day two
people arrived and proceeded to put little heaps of powder
here and there 'with ancillary mutterings'. They returned
three times at intervals of three days, and after they departed
finally, no more curious noises were heard and henceforth Mr

Sinclair's reply to all enquiries about his 'poltergeist' was the single word—'rats'.

The following week a letter from Mrs Mabel S. Smith, written from Sheringham, appeared in the *Church Times* over the signature 'G. Eric-Smith'. (Apparently Mrs Smith had decided to add her husband's Christian name to his surname to form a double-barrelled one.) It said that the writer had read with interest the preceding article and letter and went on to say: '. . . as I was in residence for some time at Borley Rectory, Sussex [*sic*] ('the most haunted house in England') I would like to state definitely that neither my husband nor myself believed the house haunted by anything else but rats and local superstition. We left the Rectory because of its broken-down condition but certainly found nothing to fear there.'

(In a letter to Peter Underwood, dated 22 September 1954, Miss Ethel Bull wrote: 'All nonsense Mrs Smith making out they were not frightened, she used to shriek with fright.')

It is interesting that the letter of the Reverend C. Sinclair showed a remarkable similarity in describing the 'disturbances' at Chale Rectory and those reported at Borley. Perhaps Mrs Smith did notice this resemblance and concluded that the 'phenomena' at Borley were due at least to a considerable extent to the same causes as at Chale. It is, of course, an open question whether rats can produce 'creaks, clangings, grinding and jarring sounds' unless they possess remarkable onomatopoeic talents.

Harry Price was still alive in 1945, and when the letter appeared he made some notes as to the manner in which he intended to deal with Mrs Smith's views in his projected third Borley book, which he unfortunately did not live to complete. These are his notes:

### FACTS

(1) It was the Rev G. Eric Smith, Rector of Borley, who (June,

1929) appealed to the Editor of the *Daily Mirror* for help in quelling the ghosts, thus introducing the hauntings to the public. The News Editor of the *Daily Mirror* asked Harry Price to investigate.

(2) It was Mr Smith and his wife who supplied Price (and others) with details of the phenomena, an account of which forms the first part of *'The Most Haunted House in England'*, the published report of the Borley Rectory hauntings.

(3) For confirmation of the details of hauntings, Price's colleague, Mr S. H. Glanville, travelled specially to Ashford, Kent (where the Smiths were then living) and spent several hours in interviewing the Smiths as to what happened at the Rectory during Mr Smith's incumbency. The notes taken at this interview were incorporated in *'The Most Haunted House in England'*.

(4) At their request, four copies of *'The Most Haunted House in England'* were sent to Mr and Mrs Smith. The book met with their unstinted praise (see correspondence), with no criticism, and Mrs Smith asked Price to try to 'place' her MS of *Murder at the Parsonage*, a novel based on the hauntings. Mrs Smith states (Nov. 19, 1940) that her book is a sequel to *'The Most Haunted House in England'*.

(5) In addition to Mr Smith's recital of the manifestations to Mr Wall of the *Daily Mirror*, and descriptions, in detail to Mr Price and his secretary (see *'Most Haunted House in England'*, pp 5-10) of the same phenomena; and long accounts of the hauntings given to Mr S. H. Glanville (on several occasions), the Smiths related psychic incidents to many people in Borley. Some of these people still reside in the village. How does Mrs Smith reconcile all these facts with her statement (*Church Times*, October 19, 1945) that 'neither my husband nor myself believed the house haunted by anything but rats and local superstition'?

(6) As for 'rats', every incumbent (including Mr Smith) informed Price that no signs of rats had been seen; and Price himself, during his tenancy of the Rectory (1938-39) saw neither rats nor mice, nor any indication that these vermin infested, or had infested, the house.

(7) And as for the hauntings being based on 'local superstition', the evidence for the haunting of Borley Rectory is based on the first-hand testimony of some 200 persons (scientific, acade-

mic, and other educated and cultured witnesses) who have
visited the place. This evidence covers a period of nearly a
century.

(8) The publication of *The Most Haunted House in England*
was due largely to the importunities of the Rev G. Eric Smith
(see his letters, Aug. 7, Nov. 20, 1929; Feb. 22, March 14,
1930) who wished to have a printed report on the case.

Price had good documentary evidence to support these
notes; but there are some points in them that must be eluci-
dated and examined. Certainly there are possible normal explanations for a number of the noises and sensations reported
during the Smith occupancy of the Rectory. Nor can mice and
rats be completely excluded. In spite of Mrs Smith's statements, it is difficult to establish whether such rodents did in
fact infest the Rectory at this period—however likely it must
appear. After all, it was an ill-lit rabbit-warren of a house with
a great many rooms, passages, attics and cellars and it was
close to farm buildings. Harry Price was emphatic in maintaining that neither he nor his investigators saw any evidence
of rats or mice, yet some of the numerous investigators during
Price's tenancy *did* refer to traces of mice. One of the rectors,
Mr Foyster, mentioned a rat-trap that was placed in the hall
in January 1932—though this may have been put down because of noises that merely suggested the presence of rats. One
possible explanation is that Harry Price, satisfied that no rats
or mice were in the Rectory during *early* investigations,
assumed that there were none during the later stages. Certainly, there is evidence that even during the early days rats
did, in fact, infest the building and Mrs Smith referred to
seeing 'enormous rats' and, in particular, seeing one 'sitting
on its haunches, licking its paws'. The creatures apparently
took up their 'residence' in the kitchen and cupboards of the
house and made their presence known by scratching the
boards. Mrs Smith's conflicting statements, however, concerning practically every incident and every person connec-

ted with the Rectory during her stay, makes it difficult to place much confidence in her tale, told some twenty years after she lived there. When we checked carefully the many original photographs of the interior of Borley Rectory, we found no trace of the characteristic damage worked by mice and rats. And when Dr H. F. Bellamy with his son and a friend visited the place in October 1937, he stated: 'One feature which impressed itself on all our minds was the extraordinary quietness of the house. There never seemed to be a board creaking nor any sign of mice or rats. In fact, the silence was almost uncanny.'

There may have been other normal sources of various noises which one must consider. There was the noisy hand-pump in the covered passage of the courtyard which could produce all sorts of curious thumps and groans, audible throughout the house, especially at night time. The singular arrangement of the Rectory buildings, erected around an almost enclosed courtyard, could also bring about odd acoustic effects. Someone walking across the courtyard, for instance, could sound sometimes as if the person were in the next room —at least to the listener inside the Rectory.

Nothing is left of the house, so this is something no one can prove or disprove today—and the ear is just as easily deceived as the eye. Nor have the sceptics insisted on using the acoustic conditions as conclusive proof of hallucination or trickery. Many of the footsteps reported to have been heard inside the Rectory quite obviously did not originate in the courtyard—for the simple reason that the courtyard itself was under observation at the time. The late Sidney Glanville, who prepared all the plans and took many of the photographs for Harry Price's Borley books (in addition to providing much of the information) and with whom we spent many hours discussing the Borley haunting, was certainly not aware of this alleged sound effect.

There was a further suggestion—that many of the curious

sounds originated in the cottage some twenty-five yards away. Some critics have suggested that the cottage (which was empty during the Smith incumbency) would with its 'adjoining gate and on the main roadway . . . not inconceivably offer shelter to passing lovers and roadfarers'; the same critics maintain that 'sibilant whisperings' or the dramatic 'Don't, Carlos, don't!' which Mr Smith reported, could have an entirely normal origin. The road through Borley is not exactly a 'main roadway'—yet the theory has a certain attractiveness, though it would be difficult to establish how many 'lovers and road-farers' would venture through two gates and trespass so close to a large occupied house. And if they did, their 'sibilant whisperings' would either have to penetrate two stout outer walls and some five rooms and seven inner walls, or travel round the L-shape of the north end of the rectory and the length of the courtyard, since, according to the Reverend G. E. Smith's testimony, he heard all this when he was just outside the Blue Room—which, as the plan of the Rectory shows—was at almost the farthest possible point from the cottage.

After nine months, on 14 July 1929, the Smiths moved out of Borley Rectory, settling down at nearby Long Melford. The reason given for their somewhat precipitate departure was the general unsuitability of the place—it was too large for two people, too primitive and under-equipped, especially as far as sanitation was concerned, with no main water and no lights—and no mention was made by either of them of any 'occult' reason. In April 1930 they made another move to Sheringham, Norfolk. Before long the Reverend Eric Smith accepted a living in Kent. Between the two dates Edwin Whitehouse (later to become Dom Richard Whitehouse) visited the Smiths in Norfolk. In January 1932 Price was still in correspondence with Mr Smith about Borley.

The Reverend G. E. Smith died on 3 August 1940. Apart from her letter to the *Church Times* in October 1945, Mrs

Smith also wrote to the *Daily Mail* some two-and-a-half years later (in May 1948, just two months after Price's death) re-asserting her disbelief in the Borley hauntings, but subsequently made no public statement.

The discrepancies between her attitude at the time of her living in the Rectory and some sixteen or nineteen years later are clear enough. As for the motive for these differences, we have indicated one or two possibilities—but it is for the reader of this book to make up his mind about the validity of these conclusions.

# 3

# *The Mysteries of Marianne*

After the Smiths departed, the Rectory was empty for six months. Then, on 16 October 1930, the Reverend Lionel Algernon Foyster, a cousin of the late Harry Bull, having been appointed to the living, moved in with his wife, Marianne, very much his junior, and an adopted daughter, Adelaide, aged 2½. The Foysters were to stay for five years, and during their stay the alleged phenomena reached an extraordinary intensity and developed a considerable variety— attracting, at the same time, a good deal of attention and criticism.

Two months after the Smiths moved out, Harry Price was in Borley, collecting information. Among others, he interviewed a journeyman carpenter, Fred Cartwright, at Sudbury; his experiences are recounted in the next chapter. Foyster himself prepared a written record of the variety of phenomena which apparently commenced soon after he and his family arrived. By about August 1931 neighbours at Borley became interested in these happenings. They included Sir George and Lady Whitehouse and their nephew Edwin (who was to become a Benedictine monk) and Sir John and Lady Braithwaite. The attitude of these neighbours varied— some were inclined to accept the phenomena as genuine, others were less prepared to do so. At the end of September 1931 the Misses Bull visited Harry Price in London and urged him to visit Borley again after an interval of some fifteen months. They also spoke to their cousin, for on 1 October 1931 the Reverend Lionel Foyster wrote to the psychic investigator and formally invited him to visit them. Some eight days later Mr W. H. Salter, later a president of the Society for Psychical Research, called on the Foysters. He had apparently heard of Price's impending visit and took it upon himself to advise Foyster (as Robert J. Hastings put it in his *Examination of the 'Borley Report'*): 'If Price's visit cannot be averted . . . get him to sign a statement against any form of publicity.' He also offered the services of the SPR 'if they should be needed'.

Foyster apparently did not take this well-meant advice, for on 13 October he welcomed Price with a party of visitors, consisting of Mrs Henry Richards, Mrs K. M. Goldney, Miss May Walker and Mr James Ballantyne, the chauffeur. Mrs Richards and Mrs Goldney were both on the Council of Price's National Laboratory of Psychical Research. Arrangements were made for the party to stay at the Bull Hotel in Long Melford.

The visit was a truly extraordinary one, for it produced a number of phenomena and led to an argument between Price and the Reverend Lionel Foyster which constituted practically a final break between the director of the NLPR and the Rector of Borley. Yet Price's record of this occasion in the Borley books did not make any mention of this break; he simply recorded the events and cautiously suggested his own scepticism in connection with them. Of course, he was limited by the libel laws of England and his own reluctance to dismiss the Borley hauntings as hallucination or fraud.

On his first acquaintance with the Foyster family, Price found the Rector a 'delightful, much-travelled and cultured person', a Cambridge MA who had been abroad in Canada from 1910 to 1929. His wife, Marianne, was 'bright, vivacious and intelligent' and also quite pretty. Her husband obviously doted on her. There were now two children in the house:

Adelaide, then $3\frac{1}{2}$, and a boy of similar age, the child of a friend, who was staying with the Foysters. A young maid of $14\frac{1}{2}$ whom the family had engaged about a fortnight before slept in a room adjoining the Blue Room.

After a long chat with their host and hostess, Price's party made the usual thorough investigation of the house, examining all doors, windows and fastenings. It became evident to Price, who had been there before, that many improvements had been made, including better sanitation, an indoor water system and extensive structural repairs. The room over the porch had been turned into a private chapel with altar, altar-rail and stained-glass window.

After making the rounds, Price and his companions returned to the ground floor for supper. Although the Foysters had prepared refreshments, Mrs Richards also contributed the contents of a luncheon basket, including a bottle of burgundy and one of sauterne. According to Price's account, he drew the corks of the two bottles and handed the burgundy to Mrs Foyster who poured a quantity into a glass. (In a letter dated 8 July 1956, almost twenty-five years after the event, Mrs Foyster stated that she never drank wine, there were no wine glasses in the house and that she passed ordinary tumblers to Harry Price who poured out the burgundy.) Whoever did the pouring, the ruby Chambertin turned to jet-black ink. Only the wine in that first glass was affected. Meanwhile Miss Walker, who was dispensing the sauterne, discovered that it smelled like eau-de-cologne.

Understandably startled, the members of the supper party carefully examined the bottles and glasses but found no solution to the mystery. But whoever or whatever was responsible for this episode, it had extraordinary and most confused consequences. According to Mr Hastings, Price considered the whole business a trick for which the hosts were responsible and told the Reverend Lionel Foyster so—which led to their parting on bad terms. Mrs Goldney hardly referred to the whole incident in the SPR report of which she was co-author-ess. As we have seen before, Mrs Smith later claimed that the whole 'drink-into-ink' affair happened much earlier, at a dinner she gave at Borley at which Price was present. If this really took place, Mrs Smith was the only person who ever recorded it—for no trace of any mention can be found in Price's files, Foyster's writings, the *Locked Book* compiled by Mr Glanville, or anywhere else. Did the same thing happen twice? The whole procedure is strongly reminiscent of a rather ordinary magician's trick. Price, of course, was a highly trained amateur magician, but if he performed such a trick why did he accuse the Foysters of it? If he had wanted to make it a valid 'phenomenon', he should have been the last man to cast doubt upon the genuineness of the event.

Soon afterwards Mrs Foyster complained of feeling unwell (she had apparently some slight heart-trouble); her husband and Mrs Goldney helped her to bed. When they rejoined the party, it was decided to examine the Rectory again. When the investigators reached the door of the study, they heard a crash and an empty claret bottle was found to have been hurled down the well of the staircase, smashing on the iron stove. At the same time one of the bells with an upstairs pull started to ring violently. Led by Mr Foyster, the whole group rushed up to find Mrs Foyster 'snug in bed': she had heard the crash and had wondered what had happened. All the upstairs rooms were then examined but everything appeared to be nor-mal. Only little Adelaide was awake; she had also heard the noises.

The party then descended to the lower floor by the back staircase. A further outburst of bell ringing and some small pebbles rattling down the stairs welcomed them back to the study, followed by the voice of Marianne calling from up-stairs. She was now locked in her bedroom. She said that first one door leading into another bedroom and then the door opening onto the landing had 'suddenly locked themselves'.

The keys to these rooms had previously disappeared, together with others. Mr Foyster produced a relic of the Curé d'Ars (the French priest who lived between 1786 and 1859 and was canonised in 1925) which he habitually carried on his person in a sachet. He and Price knelt outside the door, Mrs Foyster knelt just inside; the Rector recited a reliquary prayer. The whole party then joined in, saying the Lord's Prayer, and a sudden 'click' marked the unlocking of the door. Soon afterwards another glass object dropped down the stair-well and also smashed on the iron stove.

This was the end of the visit of Price and his party on that particular night. When they got back to the Bull at Long Melford, it was well past one in the morning. They had a discussion about the events they had witnessed and agreed that every serious 'incident' had occurred when Mrs Foyster was not within sight or under the control of the visitors. On the other hand, with the exception of the transformation of the wine, all the incidents witnessed had been reported many times previously and had been witnessed by a number of people. In the end the investigators decided to visit Borley again next morning and tell the rector frankly about these doubts.

Miss Walker returned to London early next day, but Price, Mrs Richards and Mrs Goldney called again at the Rectory. As gently as he could, Price told Mr Foyster that his wife *could* have produced the manifestations normally on the previous evening. Marianne was present at this confrontation and firmly denied that she was in any way responsible. It appears that Mrs K. M. Goldney 'intervened on her behalf' while the rector pointed out that ever since the place had been built every occupant of the Rectory had been subjected, at one time or other, to similar charges. He suggested that the visitors should spend another night at Borley, confine the whole household to one room and see what happened. This proposal was accepted. Price's group spent the rest of the day

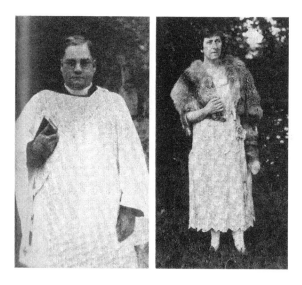

at Cambridge, returning to the Bull in time for an early dinner and then went back to the Rectory at eight o'clock.

The young nursemaid who lived in the village was sent
home and the two children were asleep in their rooms. The
grown-ups—the Rector, his wife, Mrs Richards, Mrs Goldney,
Price and Ballantyne—sat round the kitchen fire and waited.
All doors and windows in the house had been locked and
sealed. After about an hour's interval, a bell sounded in the
hall passage. It was established that it was connected with
the upstairs room occupied by Adelaide, who was found to
be awake in bed. It appears reasonable to suggest, however,
that she may have been awakened by the sudden entry of
the party into her bedroom. Price had previously noted that
the bell-pull in the room was broken off close to the ceiling;
he stated that in his view it would have been impossible for
the little girl to have pulled it, even if standing on a chair.
On the other hand, no one could have entered the room without disturbing the seals. This was the only incident recorded
that evening, for some visitors arrived a little later and further
investigation became impossible.

One result of this confused and inconclusive episode was
that Price was discouraged from visiting Borley for a considerable time. Three months after the visit, he wrote to the
Reverend G. Eric Smith, a little plaintively:

> ...Yes, some curious things have been taking place at Borley
> during the last twelve months. Two or three of us went down by
> car a few weeks ago and stayed two nights. Bottles were thrown
> at us, ink mixed with wine etc., etc. I formed a conclusion as to
> who was doing these things but of course we had no proof. I
> should like to go down there again but the Foysters will not
> permit it.

It was not until some seven years later, in about April 1939,
that good relations were restored between the psychic investigator and the Foysters. This came about through the tactful

and patient intercession of the late S. H. Glanville. By then the Foysters had been out of Borley for three-and-a-half years. The former incumbent of the Rectory gave Price permission to quote from his manuscript, 'Fifteen Months in a Haunted House' in *'The Most Haunted House in England'* which was published in August 1940.

These sections of Price's book give a condensed and sometimes carefully noncommittal account of the experiences of the Foysters, real or imaginary, and are highly revealing as to both the events and the characters of the principals involved. According to Foyster's unpublished manuscript, the 'disturbances' reached a new, previously unknown intensity and scope, including entirely new manifestations of messages and scribbled words found on walls and scraps of paper. These 'wall writings' occupied a good many people with a love of and penchant for cryptography and led to the construction of the most elaborate theories about the origins and nature of the Borley hauntings.

The incidents reported during the five years of the Foyster incumbency included a voice calling Marianne's name; footsteps heard by the Rector, his wife, little Adelaide and a workman busy in the house; the appearance of 'Harry Bull', wearing a dressing-gown which the villagers recognised from Mrs Foyster's description as one of the former rector's favourite articles of clothing; the disappearance and reappearance of jugs and other utensils and articles; strange smells, especially one resembling lavender; the ringing of bells—and even physical assault. Marianne was reported to have been given a black eye by an invisible attacker as she passed a landing; on another occasion she was struck on the head. Adelaide received a bruise which she said she had been given by a 'nasty thing' near the curtains in her bedroom. The Rector was once hit on the shoulder by a flying stone but not with any force. Sometimes articles hurtled through the air; on one occasion when a lamp was lit, the throwing stopped. An old lamp and a saucepan were set up in a curious combination outside Mr Foyster's study; a paint-pot was placed behind the door of the bedroom of a visitor known as Mr François d'Arles. Stones were also thrown on several occasions—once in the presence of a visiting bishop who was 'quite convinced that no human agency was responsible'. Pictures were found taken from the walls and laid on the floor. Objects appeared inexplicably—including a china powder-box and a wedding ring. (The latter disappeared the following morning.) Clean linen was moved and trailed over the ground. A kitchen table was found upside down and the contents of a store-cupboard scattered. There were other displacements of furniture, including a chair which was twice thrown over in a room in which Mrs Foyster lay, suffering from an indisposition; a milk-jug became emptied mysteriously and so did a saucepan of potatoes. There were many instances of doors locking themselves and of strange noises.

Nine months after their moving in and some seven months before Price's visit, things were already so harassing that Mr Foyster invited two Anglican priests to see what they could do and on 11 March 1931 they went over the house with incense and holy water, attempting a mild form of exorcism. A couple of months later the house was fumigated with creosote. None of this had any lasting effect. Mediums and spiritualist groups were also involved in trying to 'placate' whoever or whatever was causing all these disturbances—to very little avail.

The first messages that appeared in the Rectory were indecipherable and were scrawled on pieces of paper. Many of them disappeared subsequently and were then 'reproduced' on walls throughout the place.

On one occasion Marianne claimed to see the ghost of Harry Bull while she was going upstairs to get a book. As her husband recounted in his typescript, which covered the years 1930-2, she fancied that she heard a step behind her, looked

round and saw 'him' following her. She rushed into the bedroom, picked up the book she had come for and began
cautiously to retrace her steps; the figure had disappeared.
She told her husband that she had previously seen the same
figure several times and that he always wore a 'peculiar, plum-
coloured dressing-gown'. He was also seen between the library
and the Foysters' bedroom, that is, either in the hall or on
the stairs or on the landing at the head of the stairs. Occasionally Marianne said that she saw 'Harry Bull' when her husband was present—but he saw nothing. Once little Adelaide
was with Mrs Foyster when the 'phantom appeared' and the
child exclaimed 'Oh, look!' but Marianne stated that it was
impossible to say whether this exclamation referred to the
'presence' or not. A few weeks before one Christmas Mrs Foyster was alone in an upstairs sitting-room in the evening
when she heard heavy footsteps—evidently masculine—on the
stairs. Thinking that it must be her husband, she went to the
head of the stairs to meet him—only to find 'Harry Bull' facing her across a few feet. She ran back into the sitting-room
and closed the door behind her.

Visitors to the Rectory at this period also saw 'Harry Bull'
in his favourite dressing-gown at one of the windows. In 1954
Mr Foyster's brother told Peter Underwood that on one occasion when the rector was out of the house, a woman acquaintance called to see him. Marianne told her that her husband
was out, whereupon the caller said: 'You must be mistaken;
I saw him in an upstairs room—he was wearing a dressing
gown'. The younger Mr Foyster met this woman himself and
discussed the incident with her in the company of Professor
Cook of Cambridge in 1936.

It seems unlikely that Marianne could have known of the
late Harry Bull's preference for that plum-coloured dressing
gown—she had, of course, never met him—until she received
confirmation that he regularly wore it when she first told the
story of the 'apparition'. Some critics have described the for-

mer rector's numerous 'visits' as purely subjective hallucinations, the figments 'of a disordered imagination' which they ascribed to Marianne. Harry Price himself was unaware of this particular element in the history of the hauntings.

In June 1931 Edwin Whitehouse, whom we have mentioned before and who was staying with his uncle and aunt at Arthur Hall, Sudbury, visited the Rectory for the first time. There followed some thirty other visits during the next six months. His experiences included unexplained movement of objects, the appearance of 'messages', a mysterious fire in which a skirting-board was found smouldering in an unused room; door-lockings; unexplained bell-ringing (sometimes while he actually watched the bell-pulls) and the curious appearance and disappearance of bottles. On one occasion when he, Marianne and a maid, Katie, were all present, a bottle poised itself in mid-air within a foot or so of the kitchen ceiling and, after a second or two, fell with a crash to the floor. In public and private statements—among others to Peter Underwood—Whitehouse said that he had 'seen more than enough to convince him that the phenomena at Borley Rectory were preternatural'; he also asserted that after six months of observation he never had any occasion to suspect any member of the household of trickery.

The personal friends of the Foysters, Sir George and Lady Whitehouse, also had first-hand experience of the 'disturbances', both before and during the Foyster incumbency. They were friendly with the Bull family, too, and often heard the Reverend Harry Bull speak of the 'Nun' and other apparitions. Sir George died in March 1931 but his widow readily assented to a meeting with Price (this was arranged by Glanville in April 1939) and agreed that her testimony should be published by him. She explained that it was not until May 1931 that she and her husband had themselves witnessed some manifestations. While they had heard of the 'terrible experiences' of the Foysters, it was only then that, being shown the contents of a cupboard in the kitchen that had been scattered, they heard bells ringing. Marianne thought this was a warning of a 'bad time that night'. It was arranged that Sir George and Lady Whitehouse should return to the Rectory after dinner and 'see the Foysters through the evening'. They arrived about nine o'clock. The two children were in bed, asleep. The four adults sat in the kitchen while the Foysters related their ordeal in full and showed some of the scraps of paper with curious messages that had been found all over the house.

Later Sir George and Mr Foyster set out on a tour of the house but returned to report 'a strange smell'. They set out again, only to return with the news that the smell was stronger. Lady Whitehouse and Mrs Foyster then left the kitchen and Marianne at once exclaimed 'It's a fire!'

As she picked up a lamp and led the way upstairs, they all followed her along a passage to the right where there was a strong smell of burning. Marianne began to unlock the doors. As she opened the third, smoke billowed out. A strip of the skirting was seen to be smouldering with a glowing hole in the middle. Jugs of water were quickly poured on the smouldering woodwork and then, as they stood watching to make sure that the fire was out, a flint, the size of a hen's egg, fell among them. Sir George picked it up and put it in his pocket. The window of the room was shut; there was no hole in the ceiling. On the way downstairs two more flints fell, one hitting Mr Foyster a glancing blow on the shoulder. Lady Whitehouse had brought some dried lavender with her from Arthur Hall and, as it had been found that incense and sweet odours sometimes quietened things, some of the lavender was scattered on to glowing embers scooped up on a shovel and taken through the house in an attempt at fumigation. While they were passing through the Foysters' bedroom, a shower of small stones fell all round Lady Whitehouse and Mr Foyster who carried out this simple exorcism. Later a large flint hurtled down the stairs by the back door and the bells started to ring. Sir George and Lady Whitehouse decided that the house was unfit to be inhabited that night. At half-past eleven the Foysters and the sleeping children were taken to the Whitehouse home where they stayed for several days.

In the summer of the same year (1931) when Edwin Whitehouse was staying at his uncle's place, a message arrived at Arthur Hall about eleven o'clock in the morning. It was sent by Mr Foyster who asked Mr Whitehouse to come to the Rectory at once. He did so, returning about three in the afternoon and, after describing 'the ghastly time' the Foysters were having, implored his aunt to invite the Rector and his family for another stay. Lady Whitehouse went with her nephew to the Rectory. As they opened the front door, they could hear objects being thrown about. They found the children cowering near the dining-room door, saying they 'didn't like so many things falling about'. Mrs Foyster was ill in bed. Lady Whitehouse went up to her room and tried to persuade her to move to Arthur Hall for a while. She placed her gloves and parasol on the bed and went to collect some clothes for Mrs Foyster and the children. As she left the room, Marianne called out that 'her things were going'; Lady Whitehouse turned back to find her gloves and parasol transferred to the dressing-table. After she had fetched Marianne a cup of tea, a small glass bottle seemed to rise from the middle of the room and fall at her feet. When she left the room again, she heard Mrs Foyster call out and turned to find her lying on the floor—the third time such a thing had happened on that day. Soon the family was at Arthur Hall again. Lady Whitehouse added that she and Sir George had never questioned the truth of whatever they were told, and she always felt that her sympathy was 'a great help to the Foysters'. Although subsequent manifestations were often unpleasant and intensive, she and her husband never had any further personal experiences in spite of many later visits to the Rectory.

In the SPR critical survey of the Borley haunting, Dr Ding-

wall, Mrs K. M. Goldney and Mr T. H. Hall paid considerable attention to the alleged paranormal incidents during the
Foyster incumbency. One of the points they made was that,
immediately before returning to England, the Reverend L.
A. Foyster had been Rector of Sackville, Nova Scotia, described by the three analysts as being 'five miles from Amherst'. Now the latter place was the scene of the 'Great
Amherst Mystery' and much was made of the similarities the
three authors discovered between this 'classic' case of haunting and the Borley Rectory case.

There were parallels between the ages of the principal
figures in both affairs. Marianne Foyster of Borley and Esther
Cox of Amherst were both subject to spells of ill-health and
inclined to emotional outbursts. The disturbances lasted fourteen months in Amherst, fifteen months in Borley. In both
cases there are reports of apparitions, voices, objects being
moved and thrown, furniture upset; many incidents involved
beds and bedclothes, there were small outbreaks of fire, sensational 'objective phenomena'—and the protagonists of both
locations compiled diaries of the events. It was suggested as a
not-unreasonable hypothesis that the Foysters could or would
be familiar with the story of the Great Amherst Mystery and
that the Rector of Borley had read Walter Hubbell's book,
*The Haunted House: A True Ghost Story, Being an Account
of the Mysterious Manifestations that have taken place in the
Presence of Esther Cox . . . The Great Amherst Mystery*
(Saint John, New Brunswick, 1879).

Certainly, there were many similarities between the Cana-
dian and the English case. Harry Price himself cited the Amherst case in his *The End of Borley Rectory*. It is perhaps
important to bear in mind that the Amherst disturbances
were reported as being primarily linked to Esther Cox. A
young woman of nineteen, she had been the victim of attempted rape in the woods; this episode was not infrequently put
forward as a possible indirect cause of the mysterious occur-

rences. But there were also many differences between the two cases. At Amherst a box repeatedly jumped with violent force into the air; Esther herself 'visibly swelled' in the presence of five people; her pillow was several times moved in an inexplicable way in the presence of the family doctor. She was personally threatened; heavy pounding was heard from the roof and the attacks came at regular intervals of twenty-eight days. Nothing comparable happened at Borley. Amherst is a much larger place; at the time of the disturbances the population was around 3,500. The scene of the curious events was the tidy little cottage of one Daniel Teed, shoemaker, described as a neat, two-storey, yellow-painted house with bright geraniums in the window—very unlike the sprawling Borley Rectory.

In his typed record of the Borley events, Mr Foyster actually used the name Teed as one of the pseudonyms he chose for disguising the real identity of the characters. Teed was Esther Cox's brother-in-law; the critics suggested that this was an unusual name and that the Reverend Foyster used it either deliberately or subconsciously. However, it is a fairly common surname in Canada and Amherst was not all that close to Sackville, the distance being nearer ten rather than five miles 'as the crow flies'. The other names Foyster picked for his 'Fifteen Months in a Haunted House' included Buttle, Tuke, Lawless, Greycastle, Rix, Snow and Footman—certainly not as common as Brown, Black, White or Smith might have been. Finally, Amherst is situated not in Nova Scotia but in New Brunswick.

The Great Amherst Mystery had occurred more than thirty years before Foyster set foot in Canada. Except for those interested in the subject, few people would remember it; according to the check we made, neither the Rector nor Marianne was ever known to refer to the case, neither while in Canada nor during the Borley years nor afterwards. Foyster did not mention it in any of his various writings.

These writings can be divided into four items, and it may be useful to quote Mr Hastings' summary of them:

*Writing A* The original records covering the whole period of the Foyster incumbency. Claimed by Mr Foyster to have been written as a diary between February and July 1931. These writings are not in the Harry Price Library but there are references from which their sometime existence can be inferred.

*Writing B* Enlargement of Writing A for the period up to July 1931. Written in narrative form intended for circulation among members of Mr Foyster's family. In three parts, viz: (1) 'Memorandum of our experiences in connection with the Borley "Ghost" '; (2) ' "Borley Ghost"—2nd instalment'; and (3) ' "Borley Ghost" —3rd instalment'. Mr Foyster has referred to these writings comprehensively as 'Diary of Occurrences'. Original typescript in the HPL, copy in SPR files.

*Writing C* An account using pseudonyms, entitled 'Fifteen Months in a Haunted House' written with a view to publication. In a letter to Price dated 10/10/40 (HPL) Mr Foyster says that in this account he has very thoroughly camouflaged the place and the people mentioned even to the extent of changing the sex of some of the latter, and he has invented imaginary conversations, but he insists that the psychic phenomena reported in this writing are 'all exactly as they happened to the best of my knowledge and belief, and that most of them were recorded very soon after their occurrence—not seen through a distant haze of memory'. Original typescript acquired by Price for HPL at some date subsequent to the publication of *The End of Borley Rectory.*

*Writing D* Tabulated summary of experiences by Mr Foyster at Price's request in 1938 for inclusion in *'The Most Haunted House in England'*. Appears to have been abstracted from Writing A (MS in HPL).

Price's critics have objected that he published the last-named as *Leaves from the Foyster Diary* when in reality it was a summary. But the rector himself used the term 'diary' and Price simply followed suit. This, however, is one of the very minor criticisms levelled at the Foysters' account. To put it briefly, it has been repeatedly said that *all* the phenomena were engineered by Marianne for highly personal and not at all creditable reasons. Nor can the Borley events in the years 1931-5 be evaluated properly without dealing with the background and substance of these charges.

Midway through the Foyster incumbency, Canon H. Lawton spent a month in 1933 at Borley with his family while substituting for Mr Foyster. He described the Rector at that time as a man of about sixty, badly crippled with arthritis, much liked and respected in the neighbourhood. (Mrs Foyster, in 1956, contradicted this; according to her, her husband was not at all popular.) Marianne, Canon Lawton said, was then between twenty-five and thirty, physically attractive and apparently in excellent health. Major Douglas-Home stated that her health was 'superb'. Some writers criticised the fainting fits and other signs of ill-health which witnesses reported on various occasions as simulation. In his typescript essay, 'No Ghosts at Borley?', Mr R. F. Buckley pointed out that the statements about her health were highly conflicting. Price seemed to think that she was quite fit but subject to fainting fits and 'trances'. The authors of the SPR critique state: 'it is clear that she suffered from ill-health or pretended to do so', although elsewhere they quote opinions that she was 'in excellent health', 'extremely vital and healthy', 'her health was superb'. Well, we all have our off days, but it is difficult to reconcile these contradictions. She has certainly survived her husband (at this writing) by more than thirty years.

Foyster's will, made in October 1922 at Drummond, New Brunswick, named his wife as sole beneficiary. The score or so witnesses whose evidence we have obtained about the Foyster period at Borley were all emphatic in their conviction of the integrity of the rector. Nor does he appear to have been the kind of man who could be hoodwinked for five long years. His writings, too, suggest an honourable man and we see no reason to refuse acceptance of his testimony as reporting, to the best of his ability, the disturbances that were taking place. When the Reverend L. A. Foyster died at Dairy Cottages, Rendlesham, in April 1945, Marianne and he had been married at least twenty-three years. In August 1945 she married Robert Vincent O'Neil, a bachelor of twenty-nine, at Ipswich. In her signed application for the special licence, she stated that both parties were living at 229 Ranelagh Road, Ipswich, and gave her age as thirty-two. She was actually forty-six, so this statement was an obvious falsehood. It is a generally accepted feminine privilege to clip years off one's age, but Marianne used the 'clippers' somewhat excessively. This mis-statement of her real age was, of course, used against her by the challengers of the Borley hauntings, employing the argument that if a woman lied about one thing she very likely would lie about many others. This is not very good logic, but an attractive argument.

Was Marianne genuinely psychic? In a letter dated 2 September 1937, Mr Foyster told Mr S. H. Glanville that his wife possessed this quality to a high degree. The critics of the Borley hauntings claimed that the suggestion of Marianne's mediumistic talents, making her a focus of violent poltergeist activities, was not confirmed by those neighbours of hers whom they interviewed at Ipswich, Snape and Rendlesham, the places where she lived successively after leaving Borley in 1935. None of those witnesses 'even hinted' that there was anything extraordinary about her in a psychic sense, but this fact is hardly conclusive. In 1933 Marianne became part-proprietor of a flower shop in London and for about eighteen months spent five days of the week at her work, returning to Borley for the weekends. Her partner was Mr François d' Arles, whom we have mentioned before. In her letter, dated 3 July 1956, she pointed out that unexplained things were still happening at Borley while she was in London.

The authors of the SPR examination of the Borley case tried but failed to locate Marianne while writing their report. It was Peter Underwood who managed to discover her whereabouts, finding also that she had once again been widowed. She was little inclined to take an active part in any re-examination of the Borley hauntings, perhaps for understandable reasons. Thus there had been no chance of confronting her with the conclusions of Dr Dingwall, Mrs Goldney and Mr Hall, whose report suggested an 'unusual' personality, guilty of absolute and wilful trickery, inspired by the wish to leave the lonely Rectory because of boredom, frustration and unhappiness. To this they added the desire for attention from interesting people and other, less creditable motives.

It has been suggested that Marianne hated Borley and wanted to leave, but we have not come across a single statement or note from any source that she at any time expressed dislike for Borley or had ever asked her husband to leave; she was, of course, accused by Price of having produced the phenomena during that group visit in 1931. Price himself seemed to have changed his mind about her when, through Glanville, he met the Whitehouses and heard their testimony. On 27 April 1939 Price wrote to Dom Richard Whitehouse:

> . . . my mind has changed considerably since the last time I was at the Rectory (I mean when the Foysters were in residence), in view of what my observers and I have seen there since. I am now quite friendly with the Foysters, and he has kindly given me permission to reproduce what portions of his diary I think fit.

There are, of course, several possibilities suggested by this change of mind. Price might have decided that while the phenomena that occurred in 1931 during his visit were suspect, others—as described by the Whitehouses—were not. After all, he had considerable experience of mixed mediumships, of partly genuine and partly fraudulent psychic phenomena. Or, as his detractors have suggested, had he become a 'willing accomplice' of Marianne for the sake of obtaining her husband's contribution to his forthcoming book on Borley? Yet, as he pointed out in a letter to Gordon Glover, dated 11 March 1938, in his view the 'Foysters play a very small part—as far as we are concerned—in the Borley story'. And there is the third possibility that the phenomena were throughout genuine, though they did not occur under anything approaching satisfactory control—but then, few poltergeist phenomena do.

We have spent a considerable amount of time on the detailed study of the alleged paranormal happenings during the Foyster incumbency; have collected evidence from members of the families concerned and from many other people. The verdict must be a general 'not proven'—meaning that while the evidence for some alleged phenomena is far from strong, the reported incidents cannot be dismissed quite so easily and cavalierly as some critics have dismissed them.

Marianne herself wrote in her letter of 3 July 1956: 'There were a great many things which he [her husband] and I went through which no one can explain away'. She was even more explicit in the last passage of the same letter:

> ... This is a disjointed letter and one which is not probably what you wanted. If you mean did I haunt the place, the answer is No. And there is nothing and no one going to make me say I did, not all the pressure because of life can make me. That is all I have to say. America has been good to me. I work and eat and folk like me. I have a house and a garden and can go wherever I please.

It is certainly instructive, in the light of this letter, written a quarter of a century after the events, to look at the various charges and countercharges centring on Marianne and her husband.

On one occasion an 'unexplained' smell of lavender was reported in the Foysters' bedroom. Then a bag of lavender, never seen before, was found by Marianne. A few days after it had 'disappeared', the Rector found it in his coat pocket in the bedroom. The critical comment that it was 'curious' Foyster failed to see the connection between an 'apparently paranormal smell of lavender' and the physical presence in the bedroom of a bag of the same substance. Nor had Mr Foyster, it was pointed out, connected the smell of cooking reported at late hours with the Mitchells, the occupants of the nearby cottage at the time. Foyster himself dismissed this possibility, as the window of the Blue Room was on the opposite side of the house. The critics retorted that the *door* of the Blue Room was opposite the landing window overlooking the courtyard; yet this is still a considerable distance for cooking smells to travel, as the Borley map indicates.

The Reverend L. A. Foyster spoke of a 'monstrosity' which his wife and others saw near the kitchen door. Marianne, as he stated, was reluctant to tell him about the incident—as also about other happenings. (It might be pointed out that if she was trying to get away from Borley or persuade her husband to leave she would certainly have made as much as possible of such things.) The Rector described how she was moving along the kitchen passage and had almost reached the kitchen door when she suddenly looked up and saw a 'shape just in front of her'. It had a shadowy appearance and looked more like a gigantic bat than anything else. It put out a hand and touched her on the shoulder—and the touch was 'like that of a hand of iron'. Marianne screamed. Mr Foyster added that this apparition was seen by others in the house—both before and after this occasion by other people and, once again, by his wife.

During this period, according to some critics, one hundred and three phenomena took place at the Rectory. Of these, they said, ninety-nine depended on Marianne's good faith; three were independent of her 'sincerity' but could be dismissed as due to natural causes, and one incident, independent of Marianne's honesty, could be attributed to an accident—if Foyster's account was correct. This latter incident concerned the paint pot which was either moved paranormally or placed by Mr d'Arles outside a door—for some unknown reason. Of course, an opposite view might say that this analysis was a matter of making figures fit facts and then drawing deductions from the figures so obtained. 'Ghostly' happenings were reported from Borley Rectory long before Marianne Foyster was born. She herself said in the letter we have already quoted:

> I do not know who did the haunting, it had been going on for a great many years. It was going on in the time of the Bulls, but not so bad. The real bad time started in the time of the Smiths and got so bad they left. I had two maids who left in a short time.

On 11 May 1960, the Borley haunting in general and the Foyster occupancy in particular were the subject of a Ghost Club discussion in which Dr Letitia Fairfield, CBE, MD, DPH, barrister-at-law, and Miss Christina Hole, the well-known writer and distinguished authority on witchcraft and hauntings, talked with Peter Underwood. Miss Hole had once participated in a broadcast with Harry Price about the Borley hauntings.

Dr Fairfield seemed to be impressed with the critics' case and cited some unpublished evidence regarding Marianne. (This mainly involved irregularities in her various marriages.) The answer was that these charges, proven or unproven, could make no difference to the Borley hauntings. Dr Fairfield replied that it certainly made a difference to the acceptability of the Foysters' evidence. But by and large the 'mysteries of Marianne' were recorded without much reliance being placed on them—they form part of the immensely varied and rich human tapestry that is the background of Borley. Though Harry Price changed his opinion about her and her husband to some extent (and some eight years after their first meeting), he sized her up on the first encounter and decided she could not be trusted. It was not her evidence he quoted at this time but that of her husband—and little if any doubt has been cast on the reliability of the latter. Mrs Goldney has suggested that the elderly Rector was infatuated with his young wife and that therefore whatever he said or wrote must be discounted because of this; that all he put on paper was sheer supposition, unaccompanied by any facts. Equally, we have no real evidence that Mr Foyster was so 'bewitched and besotted'. The incidents he recounted in his manuscript, 'Fifteen Months in a Haunted House', have a certain ring of truth; he was careful to underplay and thoroughly weigh evidence that relied solely on his wife's word. Miss Christina Hole agreed that the case of the critics of the Borley hauntings was largely concerned with putting Harry Price into the dock as a sort of secondary or unconscious accomplice of Marianne —which he certainly was not. There is ample documentary proof that he was not 'fooled' or misled by her—even if for reasons of libel and other considerations he could not make his doubts public.

Edwin Whitehouse was about the same age as Marianne, with whom he appears to have been on terms of friendship and, as the critics phrased it, he was 'ready to put himself to considerable trouble to protect [her] from the criticism of sceptics'. This 'anxious and active consideration for Marianne', the critics added, may well have been the subconscious cause of the young Whitehouse's testimony being biased in favour of a paranormal explanation. Biased to such an extent that in a chapter of *'The Most Haunted House in England'* he described at least one phenomenon which he did not witness at all! It concerned a fragile tumbler which, he said, dropped near his feet, circled round him and came to rest without breaking. Whitehouse, writing to Price after the first printing of the book, said that he found a 'curious mistake' in his testimony, concerning one incident which described Marianne as being ill in the room next to the Blue Room whereas it was in fact the Blue Room itself. He added that he did not in fact witness the incident of the tumbler as he 'arrived just after it had taken place'. Price made the necessary alteration in respect of the Blue Room in reprints of his book, but not about the tumbler. The critics pointed out that Whitehouse's account of his experiences was written eight years after the events he described. Regarding a report of bottle materialisation which he *did* witness, with Marianne and a maid at the Rectory, it was pointed out that Whitehouse's testimony contained no suggestion about the bottle originating 'from a mushroom shape'. The discrepancy in the details of the incident as published in Price's two books about Borley had a very simple explanation: in the meantime additional evidence had reached him. The SPR report's authors pointed out that only a month before this 'bottle materialisation' Price had witnessed a demonstration of bottle-*throwing* and had been satisfied that Marianne had been responsible. The late Captain V. M. Deane of Braiswick, Colchester, who (like several others) studied the Borley case for many years, was quite emphatic about these bottle phenomena which we discussed with him at a meeting of the Ghost Club in 1948. Writing in *Psychic Science* (April 1941) he stated that he had cross-examined the principal witnesses 'for hours on end' and was in possession of the entire records of the sittings of the Marks Tey spiritualist circle for the twelve months of 1932 (during which they had visited Borley and held séances), and that in his belief there was not the slightest shadow of doubt: bottles and stones fell at Borley Rectory in full lamp-light among groups of three to five witnesses who saw, heard and handled them.

Bottles certainly played a large part in the phenomena reported during the Foyster occupancy, although, curiously enough, apart from the manifestations during a visit by the Marks Tey circle, only two small incidents concerning them were mentioned in Mr Foyster's manuscript account. It is in-disputable that many incidents involving bottles did occur; this omission perhaps showed that (as the Rector was care-ful to point out) his account did not profess to be a precise record of all the alleged phenomena during the five years he and his family spent at Borley. He did not mention the 'wine-into-ink' episode nor the appearance of the pendants—but this, however vividly dramatised by one critical report, should not be given an exaggerated importance. Bottles were reported to have been repeatedly 'apported' into Borley Rec-tory. Sceptics offered the explanation of faulty observation and false testimony to explain them—others might prefer a less negative interpretation.

Here it is interesting to recall that, a few weeks before the Smiths moved into the Rectory in October 1928, Mrs Smith found one of the cellar doors locked. When she asked a gar-dener about this, she was told that 'to his knowledge' the door had been opened and that part of the cellar was found to be piled high with empty wine bottles—so the bottles that appeared within the Rectory did not have to travel very far. (This information was given by the Smiths to Mr Glanville at Sevington Rectory, Kent, on 6 October 1937.) Bottles were also found in quantity during the various excavations of the Rectory cellars.

The local 'help' told Marianne at one time that she was tired of sweeping the broken bottles and would do so no more —whereupon, it seems, no more such bottles appeared while that particular maid worked at Borley. Mr Foyster comments on this in his manuscript:

> During the afternoon different articles were carried in and laid down in the kitchen passage. Mrs Rayner [*a misnomer*, PU & PT], our char-lady, must have spent quite a little while carrying things out, stones and various debris. I suppose she attributed it to Phyllis [Foyster's pseudonym for little Adelaide] since one after-noon she complained that 'that baby' had carried in heavy things

that she did not find easy to lift . . . there were no demonstrations while she was in the house, in her vicinity at any rate, except for bell-ringing, else we might have lost the services of a very excellent char-lady, to say nothing of having strange reports circulating in the village. The bell-ringing when it took place certainly did not worry her. On one occasion she went to the front door but no one was there. She tried the back door with the same unsatisfactory result. Presently she spied on the road a poor innocent youth returning home from school. Here undoubtedly was the culprit. 'What do you think you are a-doing of, James, ringing the bell like that? Do you think I have nothing else to do than run to the door for nothing? Wait till I tell your mother about it.' James continued on his way in mystified and injured silence!


Today it seems to be generally accepted that the 'messages', some on scraps of paper and some appearing on the walls of the Rectory—practically all of them during the Foyster incumbency—originated in Marianne, either consciously or unconsciously. The messages, which mostly had a Roman Catholic flavour, appealed for 'light', 'Mass', 'prayers' and 'help'. They included what seemed to be a number of French words and were often addressed to 'Marianne'. Frequently they were illegible; naturally, a good deal of speculation was centred upon their correct translation and interpretation. In the opinion of a distinguished graphologist, only one of the words that appeared at Borley as a message was written by a second personality—the word 'Edwin' that was noted by Mr Kerr-Pearse on 13 July 1937. According to the expert, all the rest was written by the same hand. Details of the Borley messages, including tracings, occupy ten pages of Glanville's *Locked Book*. There can be no doubt that the general tone of the messages was of great interest to Edwin Whitehouse, the future Dom Richard Whitehouse, osb. He and others agreed that even if one was inclined to accept Marianne's responsibility for the majority of them, an explanation of the origin of the impulse to write them still demanded an explanation—

and a different one from the facile interpretations offered by some critics.

These critics have pointed out that the messages all appear to have been executed during the summer of 1931 and that nothing comparable emerged at any time during the more than seventy years of the Rectory's life. It does appear that messages reported later *might* have been overlooked previously and were in fact not new writings—although some witnesses were emphatic that, in fact, they had discovered new ones a number of years later. Price, writing to Mr H. de B. Saunders on 18 March 1948, only a few days before his death said:

> As a matter of fact we have already decided that Mrs Foyster MAY have been the instrument through which the scripts appeared on the walls—I mean as a secondary personality. If so, this would NOT invalidate the veridical content of the messages.

This statement has been used by critics to discredit the whole complex of the messages—while others have cited it in support of Price's conviction of their genuineness. Here we seem to be passing from the field of the occult to that of pyschology and perhaps even psychiatry. For no one has yet given a satisfactory explanation of *why* Marianne did all this—if we accept the view that she did it.

There were considerable variations in the writing—which, Marianne's accusers said, were (or might be) due to the need for the writer to hurry on some occasions, while at other times there was no risk of detection. One message apparently turned up while Marianne was visiting the Rectory with Edwin Whitehouse and he had left her for a moment. Then, again, there were references to little Adelaide who was described as a 'terror for scribbling', apt to write and scrawl on every wall. In his manuscript account the Reverend Lionel Foyster said that, in fact, the child was just over three at the time the

messages appeared and could not yet write. Mrs Goldney told
Peter Underwood on 25 August 1950 that the little girl was
'very backward at that time'. Thus the evidence for and
against the paranormal appearance of these curious messages
and markings is reasonably evenly balanced. The late Professor C. E. M. Joad told several people (including Peter Underwood) about the night he spent at Borley with a fellow
observer. They went round the house, carefully examining
all the squiggles and 'messages'; yet, half-an-hour later, on
the wall immediately facing the door of the base-room, Joad
found another squiggle which he was certain had not been
there before. In fact, such squiggles appeared on many different occasions over a number of years; no single person could
have been responsible for all of them.

Perhaps too little notice has been taken of the size of some
of the writings and the height at which they appeared on the
walls. Sidney H. Glanville was aware of this aspect and we
discussed the matter with him on several occasions. In his
meticulously prepared *Locked Book* he was careful to give
exact details of the traced writings and scribblings he noted
and recorded for all time. Most of the more legible messages
(including the one to which Marianne added 'I cannot under-
stand . . . ') and the 'Marianne-light-mass-prayers' message
appeared at heights of around four feet six inches from the
ground; the height at which an adult could most easily write
while standing. In the 'light-mass etc' message some of the
letters were one-and-a-half inches high and the word
'Marianne' was almost seven inches in length. The 'Get light
mass and prayers' message was at a height of four feet eight
inches, with some of the letters over two inches high and the
whole message some six inches wide and over nine inches
deep. Most of the squiggles appeared at heights of two feet
three inches and two feet six inches from the ground (a height
perhaps best suited to a child); however, one appeared at a
height of four feet four inches and another at four feet from

the ground.

The SPR report pointed out that when Mr Glanville photographed the writings at Harry Price's request, he pencilled them over. The suggestion was made that Glanville was probably influenced in the transcription of at least one message by an interpretation suggested by Kerr-Pearse and that the original message was photographed differently from its original form. It was implied that the wily Price suggested to Glanville the re-touching of the writings. In fact, the suggestion that the writings should be re-touched (ie traced with pencil) to make photographing possible, came from Glanville in a letter to Price, dated 28 October 1937. In this Glanville pointed out that on one of the photographs he had taken, the wall-writing was indecipherable and he asked: '...Do you think it would be advisable to carefully bring the old writing, just visible now, up to a state where it (ie the photography) would be possible?' Price replied on 29 October 1937: '... As it is of vital importance, for the book, that we should have good photographs of the writings, I think it will be as well if you were to strengthen carefully the marks etc. so that they are photographable. May I count on you to do this?' Thus Price was simply replying to Glanville's suggestion rather than initiating the procedure. (Copies of these letters were preserved in the *Locked Book*.)

After *The End of Borley Rectory* was published in 1946, Price received a great many letters. Quite a few of them made interesting or fanciful suggestions about the interpretations of the wall-writings reproduced in the book. Thus a Mr J. P. Bessor, writing from Zelienodle, USA, wondered whether the biblical 'writing on the wall' was in any way similar to the Borley messages. C. N. Thompson, B.SC, ARIC, writing from 'Cherrybank', Aigburth Hall Avenue, Liverpool, contributed 'an impartial bystander's' view regarding the last pencilled wall message printed in *The End of Borley Rectory*. He had looked at it before reading the text and 'deciphered' it almost immediately. He was surprised to see suggestions that it might be 'Mas[s] by [Ab]bey' and 'Mas[s] by boy' or even a series of Sanskrit characters! He suggested that, done in a more normal hand, it would be merely 'Mrs Foyster'. He pointed out that the 'F' had been crossed out last and the second or lower cross was incorporated with the underlining flourish. In order to check whether he was perhaps deluding himself as to the accuracy of his interpretation, he showed a friend the reproduction of the message in the book, remarking merely that it was an unusual name. His friend's first attempt was 'Mrs Royster', the second guess was correct—and this was proposed by someone who had not read either of the Borley books! There is a strong possibility that Mr Thompson was right and that this message which has come in for so much scrutiny and examination was simply 'Mrs Foyster'—though of course the question of its origin remains unsolved.

A number of correspondents suggested that the 'odd marks' in the same message might be a hurried attempt to write '1667', given as the year of her death by a communicating entity 'Lairre' at a planchette séance to Sidney Glanville's daughter, Helen (now Mrs Carter), at their Streatham house on 28 October 1937. Lieutenant-Colonel G. M. Prynne, writing from Little Kinglet, Chagford, Devon, had some interesting observations to make on the word 'light' which appeared in the messages:

It occurs to me that for reasons which may not have been very apparent she wished for physical light in some form. I have always felt that psychical phenomena, which would seem to be most manifest during the hours of darkness, may be dependent to some extent for their necessary energy, upon light in certain conditions and circumstances. Is it possible that artificial light during darkness might have facilitated her task of writing messages, which often seem confused as they would be when written in the dark? This may all seem to be a very vague theory, though it does not appear to be unnatural that psychical phenomena and physical light, heat and energy should be clearly interdependent. Should it, moreover, prove to have some foundation, would it not possibly explain the lights seen at the Rectory? Could not they also have been 'pointers'?

Lieut-Col Prynne was here referring primarily to the 'mysterious light' reported to have been seen in the windows of Borley Rectory on many occasions. As we have mentioned before, there had been people living in Borley who recalled Mrs Smith pointing out the light to them—including Mrs E. E. Payne of Borley Place. Inevitably, it was suggested that this light was merely the reflection of passing vehicles, particularly trains. However, Mr S. F. C. Kiernander of Bramhall in Cheshire, a member of the Ghost Club, reminded us that, at the time these reports were prevalent, the Rectory was almost surrounded by high trees which would negate such an explanation. In a letter dated 6 February 1935, to Peter Underwood, Mrs Henning (widow of the Reverend A. C. Henning, Rector of Borley with Liston) stated: 'Lots of women in Borley were taken by Mrs Smith to look at the light which could not be explained'.

In the interview Lady Whitehouse gave some SPR investigators, she said that—'with certain qualifications'—she considered one phenomenon she witnessed at Borley during the Foyster incumbency, 'to be quite inexplicable'. This was the fire incident which we have already described. No one could dispute that Sir George and Lady Whitehouse were quite sincere in their conviction: Marianne could not possibly have been responsible for this incident. It was only eight years after it occurred that Lady Whitehouse was asked for her statement, though in October 1931, five months after it happened, one of the SPR investigators (Mrs Goldney) visited Borley. At that time Lady Whitehouse did not think it worth while to describe her experience. It is reasonable to conclude that, like so many other people who went to Borley, she failed to realise the extraordinary features and the importance of the

Borley case. Harry Price was probably the first to do so. (Actually, there is evidence suggesting that leading members of the SPR knew of the Borley case *before* Price but failed to investigate.)

In any case, the critics of the Borley hauntings suggested that perhaps Lady Whitehouse's recollection of the details of the incident may have become blurred. She stuck to her story, however—even though the fire incident could not have been staged by Marianne. Some of the critics, at least where Mrs Foyster could not be implicated in alleged trickery, sought to weaken the force of the testimony by others in various ways.

François d'Arles and Edwin Whitehouse were regarded by some critics—'if their stories are to be accepted'—as the only two people who witnessed visual phenomena at Borley during the Foyster incumbency, apart from Marianne herself. The critics suggested that it was stretching credulity too far to accept the coincidence of Foyster never seeing any of the appearances of the figures, bottles poised in mid-air etc during five years, while Whitehouse and d'Arles, 'fortuitously brought into contact with Borley and Marianne', were sufficiently endowed with psychic powers to share her experiences. This is an attractive argument—but the fact is that, according to documentary evidence, at least eight people testified to visual psychic phenomena during the period in question, while there is at least *some* evidence that an additional four also witnessed such happenings. One might question Marianne's own unsupported claims—but a dozen other people could hardly be ignored.

It is quite true that, once Marianne left the Rectory, nothing remotely resembling the phenomena reported during the Foyster occupancy occurred. Critics have said that unless Marianne was accepted as a passive focus for phenomena of a type and violence never duplicated at Borley over a period of seventy years before and after she lived there, she must be held responsible for faking them. This is supported by such statements as: 'Her [Marianne's] approach to the problems which beset her may have been unusual, judged by normal standards . . . '—though neither her approach nor the standards are defined. Or: 'Glanville has stated that Marianne was subject to considerable emotional outbursts, and was unconventional in the social sense.' Mr Glanville never met Marianne Foyster and he said once to Peter Underwood in the presence of Mrs Goldney: 'I'd have given my left hand to have met her . . . ' A man of high integrity, he reported the conclusions of others but never claimed them as his own.

To sum up the theory which the accusers of Marianne have developed: they suggested that the discomfort of the Rectory made her wish to leave the place while her husband considered it his duty to stay there. This, they reason, was the motive for her staging a number of objective and alarming incidents, using the traditional legend of the Rectory as a basis, trying to show her husband that life there was intolerable and even affected her health adversely. She was a pretty young woman, they add, there was that considerable age-gap between her and the rector who also suffered from chronic arthritis—so she may well have been the victim of boredom, frustration and unhappiness. Being the centre of attention from interesting people as long as the manifestations took place might well make her life a good deal more endurable. After the visit by the spiritualists in January 1932 the alleged phenomena ceased abruptly, the analysis of the sceptics continues—perhaps because suspicions against her were mounting and, following a general 'spring clean', she must have decided that the 'performance' she put on should end. Edwin Whitehouse's evidence was called 'open to considerable doubt'. As no first-hand evidence was available as to the evidence of Mr d'Arles nor was anything known about him at the time—except that he changed his name and that the Misses Bull described him once to S. H. Glanville as an 'extraordinary man'—he was also dismissed as a witness. (The

Misses Bull spoke of him to Peter Underwood as 'an odd
and peculiar man'.) Today, however, considerably more is
known about him, owing to extensive research by Mr Alan
Roper, a member of the Ghost Club and of the SPR. (This information appears in the Appendix at the end of this book.)

In October 1931 Mrs K. M. Goldney visited Borley and
met Edwin Whitehouse. He told her that he had had a nervous breakdown and, feeling in need of a holiday, had gone
to stay with his aunt and uncle at Arthur Hall, Sudbury.
There, as we have seen before, he was introduced to the Foysters and visited Borley. Lady Whitehouse herself said that
Edwin was recovering from the breakdown during the period
he witnessed the phenomena at the Rectory. Unfortunately
his recovery was not permanent and two letters from him to
Harry Price in February 1937 indicate that he was suffering
from a further 'maladjustment of some severity'. This
occurred in the period between his 1931 experiences at Borley and the preparation of his statement for 'The Most
Haunted House in England' in 1939. The phrase 'maladjustment of some severity', it should be noted, is one the authors
of the SPR critique coined and not Whitehouse's own or that
of some medical expert.

Following an approach from him, in April 1956, we exchanged several letters with Dom Richard Whitehouse and
later met him in London where Peter Underwood spent three
hours discussing Borley with him. It soon became evident that
in many respects Dom Richard had been misquoted or mis-
interpreted by the critics of the Borley hauntings. Subsequently, Dom Richard set out for us in a letter dated 6 August 1956 the main points which the three critics raised
against him and his evidence. These consisted of five main
arguments: (1) that he wrote eight years after the events he
witnessed and from memory, without any notes or contem-
porary sources; (2) that in 1931 he had just recovered from a
nervous breakdown which prejudiced his account; (3) that he

got his information regarding the so-called stiletto, bottle and tumbler incidents from Marianne and was biased in favour of a paranormal explanation; (4) that in his letter of 6 November 1940 he stated that he had *not* witnessed the tumbler incident; and (5) that Mrs Mabel Smith had no recollection of ever meeting him.

His letter of August 1956 answered all these points very fully and frankly. On the first point, he objected to the fact that the authors of the Borley report omitted any reference to his notes. His contribution to Price's '*The Most Haunted House in England*' (page 93) clearly stated: 'In my notes I have recorded the fact that on one of our visits we found a bed overturned. These observations, I repeat, were made during the period when the house was empty.' In fact, he was *keeping notes within ten days of his arrival at Borley* in June 1931 and his chapter in the Price book was based on these notes which he had preserved. On page 100 of the same book he once again referred to these notes, twice in the last two paragraphs. As for the allegation that he obtained his information at second hand from Marianne, Dom Richard suggested that there would have been no point in this concerning events which he had witnessed himself. Marianne *did* tell him that she had seen a stiletto rise from the floor and twist in the air; but he refuted the SPR interpretation of having based his 'judgement of the Borley phenomena as a whole on her story'. He accepted the paranormality of the incident— because the stiletto was levitated on to his lap while he was actually looking at Marianne who had not moved hand or foot. (It was then that she told him about the previous movement of the dagger.) As for three other incidents involving bottles which the critics did not mention and which occurred on 13 November 1931, 'these were astonishing and startling phenomena' but were described by him '*soberly and factually*'. He asserted that he would never go back 'on what I said in Chapter XV of Price's first Borley book . . .'

As to his nervous breakdown, he explained that on 1 February 1956, when she interviewed him in the presence of his abbot, Mrs Goldney reminded him of their conversation of twenty-five years before, in October 1931, during which he made a reference to a nursing home in Harrow. She did not seem to realise that this reference was to 1924-5, and in her report treated the breakdown as if it had taken place during his 1931 Borley visit. 'Mrs Goldney has already acknowledged that her memory was at fault', Dom Richard said, and added that he *was* ill in 1937 but recovered and did two or three years' hard study between then and his ordination in May 1940. When he wrote his contribution to the Price book, he was a deacon.

On the third point Dom Richard said:

> They [the Borley critics] explain the stiletto, bottles and tumbler incidents by saying in all these cases that I got my story and facts from Mrs Foyster. *I utterly repudiate this.* I hardly if ever wrote to Mrs Foyster after about 1932/33, except to submit the *finished* article on Borley in 1939 which they approved. I saw Mrs Foyster once after leaving Borley—it was in London for a short while during her flower-shop period. I did not know then that it was a partnership with De Arles [*sic*]. I went to some Convent Chapel with her on this occasion and was also shewn the flower-shop from the opposite side of the road. I cannot recall where or what part of London this was . . . *

Fourthly, Dom Richard continued, if the contention of the critics were correct, he would be denying in his letter what he affirmed positively and described as a personal experience in his published account. This would indeed prove him unreliable. Though he had committed a slight topographical error in his contribution to the Price

* It was Jonquille et Cie, 20a Worple Road, Wimbledon, SW19.

book, all the rest was totally factual. Indeed, he pointed out, Mr Foyster would have been the first to protest if he had described something as a personal experience when he was not present at a particular incident. 'In a letter', he continued, 'one does not write as if every syllable was going to be examined minutely—"arriving as I did just after it happened" just means that I arrived soon after the precipitation of objects . . . '

Mrs Smith, he stated, dealing with the five points, certainly *did* meet him. The lady apparently suffered from similar lapses of memory—for she had also denied meeting Mr Glanville. In fact, Mrs Smith showed Dom Richard at Sheringham the very dressing-table that 'became animated' and gave him no impression whatsoever that she did not believe in the phenomena at Borley. Nor was she in any way disinclined to discuss the phenomena. While women have a proverbial privilege to change their minds, Mrs Smith seemed to have had recourse to this right somewhat extensively.

Dom Richard also referred to the wall-writings about which he felt he had to reserve judgement. But the word 'light' about which so many theories were put forward presented no problem to him. He regarded it as an answer to prayer for 'special guidance' which was the intention of the Novena. If a Mass had been offered by a Roman Catholic priest at Borley, he thought, 'light', that is, guidance, would have been vouchsafed. When he wrote his letter to Price in March 1941, Dom Richard must have been influenced (so he suggested) by the part of the message that he had not seen himself in June 1931—the message which was reproduced on page 197 of the SPR report. This, he thought, might mean: 'THERE [Latin = ibi] Mass by Boy' (Dom Richard was called 'Boy' as a child by relatives).

He added that he was never convinced that the whole message or any part of it was a genuine answer to prayer; his mind wavered between the possibility of its being 'a diabolic trick' or the former. Any Catholic priest would suspect a message written in this manner. He did feel, however, that a Mass could have been offered at Borley—and 'perhaps should have been'. He had no reason to believe that Marianne had *consciously* written the message herself. He was certain that she could not have made all the bottles arrive on 13 November 1931 or dropped the tumbler on 14 December or thrown the stiletto on to his lap.

Dom Richard, before correcting some minor errors of the SPR report, summed up his views:

> I never cast suspicion on Marianne and I defended her, because I *knew* after the stiletto incident, bottles, tumbler and so forth (bells, knocks, key disappearances etc) that whatever other things —such as the pills being placed in my pocket—she *may* for some obscure reason have done *herself*, she certainly *did not* manufacture the stiletto landing on my lap, the bottles and tumbler.
>
> When one is convinced that she hadn't manufactured the *major* physical phenomena of the stiletto, bottles and tumbler I find it less likely that she would have reason to perpetrate the *lesser* things fraudulently and consciously.

Dom Richard Whitehouse was impressive as a witness and obviously sincere in his desire to discover the truth about the curious happenings at Borley during the Foyster incumbency.

In October 1935, the Reverend and Mrs Foyster left Borley Rectory, and after that date the Rectory never again housed a clerical family. Mr Foyster was, by that time, completely crippled by arthritis and spent all his time in a wheel-chair. He had suffered two bad heart attacks, and on the last occasion when he preached at Borley church he collapsed in the pulpit.

After her husband's death, Marianne seemed to disappear from sight. In the early 1950s, as we have mentioned before, she was traced in America. After the SPR report was published in January 1956, Marianne's son—whom T. H. Hall,

apparently at his own request, identified only as 'X'—approached the University of London. 'X' was obviously eager to remove the paranormal 'stigma' from his mother's past as he was strongly, even fanatically, opposed to any occult theory and practice.

In 1957 Marianne was visited by a 'legally qualified investigator' in Jamestown who, in turn, persuaded her to pay a visit to the Parapsychology Foundation in New York (headed by the late Mrs Eileen Garrett, the distinguished voice medium). There she recorded a statement on tape. In direct contradiction to the letter she wrote on 3 July 1956 (and which we have quoted), she said she did not believe in ghosts and poltergeists and that Borley was not haunted while she lived there. She stated that she never saw a monstrosity or apparition of any kind on any occasion nor had she any recollection whatsoever of any incident involving a stiletto.

This long statement was paraphrased in 1965 in Trevor H. Hall's *New Light on Old Ghosts*. Hall also conducted elaborate researches into Marianne's life—but neither the New York tape nor the result of these researches has become available for detailed study. As one of us pointed out in the SPR re-examination comprising Volume 55, Part 201, of the SPR *Proceedings*, T. H. Hall's collection on Marianne Foyster, which he presented to the Harry Price Library, was returned —'because it was felt that it was not a suitable addition to the collection and could not have been made available for consultation'.

So the mystery of Marianne is still unsolved. One is tempted to speculate about her various changes of mind, her contradictory statements, her controversial character—but this would be unprofitable. She is certainly one of the most colourful and unusual figures in the large cast of the Borley characters—and we had better leave it at that.

# 4
# *Price at Borley*

We have spoken, inevitably, of Harry Price's connection with Borley Rectory during the incumbencies of the Bulls, Smiths and Foysters, dealing with it from the point of view of those living at the Rectory. But his interest in the alleged hauntings continued long after the last of the parsons residing at Borley had left and, of course, the story must also be told from his point of view. The two books he wrote, the third he was preparing at the time of his death, the innumerable articles, broadcasts and the vast correspondence the rambling, uncomfortable house inspired were largely centred on Harry Price. His enemies and critics were likely to deny the reality of the phenomena; his friends and partisans were equally inclined to champion their genuineness. And between them there was the vast 'middle ground'—thousands who were simply intrigued and excited by the story and who were neither against nor for the claims being made, the theories being developed. Certainly some of the most bitter attacks on Harry Price's integrity and methods were unchained by Borley; equally, the most zealous defence, the most enthusiastic support, came from those who were his collaborators and admirers during the almost twenty years during which he was, on and off, concerning himself with the case. For several years he *was* the Man of Borley.

The date of Price's first visit, as we have mentioned before, was 10 June 1929. After listening to Mr and Mrs Smith's account of their experiences and the various local legends, Price and his secretary, Miss Lucy Kaye (later Mrs Meeker) made a complete tour of the Rectory. They sealed all doors and windows they could not personally control, examined the garden and outhouses and sent the maid, a local girl, home. At dusk Price and Mr V. C. Wall, a *Daily Mirror* reporter, stood by the large summer-house, and while Wall watched for the 'phantom nun' Harry Price kept a look-out for the strange light that was said to appear at an upstairs window. After about half-an-hour Wall declared that a shadow was moving along the Nun's Walk; Price thought, too, that he saw it. There was no light in the window. As it was now dark, they decided to return to the house. As they passed under the glass-topped verandah, a half-brick crashed through the roof and showered splinters upon them. They made an immediate and thorough search but could find no explanation. They re-entered the house and checked the seals, which they found intact from attics to cellars; but, as they reached the hall, a red glass candlestick hurtled down from the upper stories and smashed at their feet. (The critics of the Borley hauntings claimed that Mrs Smith never had a red glass candlestick. In fact, she stated, at a much later date, that she did not have one; but as her memory had been proved rather shaky on more important points, the testimony of Price and Wall obviously deserve more credence in this matter.)

The two men ran upstairs and found the candlestick to be one of a pair standing on the mantelpiece of the Blue Room. A further search of the house provided no clues. Then, as Price stated, they were pelted with mothballs, pebbles and pieces of slate—all seemed to originate on the first floor. Once more they conducted a fruitless search to find an explanation. Later, several of the old-fashioned bells rang without any apparent human agency. Price actually saw the bell-pulls moving but was quite unable to explain what was moving them. Then the keys of the library and dining-room simultaneously dropped to the floor. Price, an expert conjuror, immediately examined them, as well as the doors—but could not discover any normal means by which this could have been accomplished. There was no connection between the library and the dining-room, their doors faced in different but not opposite directions, so that air pressure (which some writers put forward as a possible explanation) could not have accounted for the simultaneous propulsion of the keys.

Once he had gathered some idea of the nature of the Borley phenomena, Price set out to interview the previous occupants, gathering all available details. Ably assisted by Mr Sidney H. Glanville, he obtained the evidence of the surviving members of the Bull family which we have summarised in our first chapter and which established the beginning of the haunting at a date of almost seventy years previously when the Reverend H. D. E. Bull built the Rectory. It was during this time that Price first heard about the phantom coach-and-horses and the traditional story of the eloping nun and groom (or monk). The former, alleged to have been seen in the vicinity of the Rectory, seemed to have little logical connection with the tale of the elopement but was rather an attempt to substantiate traditions. The evidence for the phantom coach (a recurrent *motif* in so many ghost stories) must be adjudged to be considerably weaker than that for the 'nunlike' figure. Mary Pearson (later Mrs Tatum) repeatedly spoke of seeing the coach during the days when she was a maid at the Rectory. Her evidence was later dismissed by Mrs Smith, who said that the maid was laughing at the time she told her employer about sighting the coach—so the Rector's wife did not think she was altogether serious. But Mrs Smith herself always claimed that late one evening, while alone at the Rectory, she heard the drive gates open. She became nervous, took a lantern and moved to a window. She saw two 'headlamps' which were extinguished while she watched. However, by the light of these lamps, she did see the outline of some sort of vehicle. When her husband came in and she questioned him, he said there was nothing in the drive. Price's original notes recorded that Mary Pearson spoke of seeing the coach on the lawn 'like a big cab' with two bay horses.

Mr Edward Cooper claimed that he saw the black coach one bright moonlit night from a bedroom window in the Rectory cottage. Two lamps which seemed to be headlights first attracted his attention, and as they drew nearer he was able to distinguish a large, old-fashioned coach which, drawn by two horses, sped rapidly past. His evidence, it must be remembered, was given only after accounts of the ghostly coach-and-pair had been published; yet country folk are naturally reserved about such matters and talk of them only when they know they will not be ridiculed. Mary Pearson also told Harry Price that she saw a man 'apparently without a head' behind a tree; by 1952 she was quoted as admitting that her statement was untrue. Suggestions have been made that this 'apparition' and other figures seen at this period were in reality one flesh-and-blood person, Fred Tatum, Mary's friend, whom she later married. Mrs Smith, in one of her later accounts of life at the Rectory in 1929, said that Fred Tatum was frequently at the place—though she knew nothing about it at the time. However, the Reverend Harry Bull had also spoken about seeing a headless figure, telling Lady White-house and others about glimpsing one in the garden, and this 'apparition' could not have been Fred Tatum—nor could those seen by Mr Edward Cooper. Mrs Lloyd Williams saw a 'round, dark object' in 1938 which she thought might have been a 'short, stooping figure'—conceivably the same phantom. All this is inconclusive personal experience rather than corroborated evidence—which, unfortunately, is rarely forthcoming in such cases.

Harry Price evidently made a mistake in relating Mr Edward Cooper's story of the phantom coach. Price reported that Cooper saw it from his bedroom window, its lamps blazing and its harness glittering in the moonlight, as it swept across the meadow by the church, passing through the hedge and into the farmyard witout any sound. In August 1954 Brigadier C. A. L. Brownlow, together with Peter Underwood, interviewed Mr and Mrs Cooper independently. It became evident by Cooper's later story that the coach was proceeding in the opposite direction. 'They got it a bit muddled in the book', Mr Cooper remarked. His later version told of his looking out one evening from his bedroom window at the back of the cottage and seeing a coach or square cab, drawn by two horses and with two side-lamps alight and the harness shining. A rather dim figure sat on the box. There was no headless coachman. Even so, Cooper was astonished at such an unexpected and amazing sight and he called to his wife to come and look. However, the 'apparition' had vanished before she answered the call. When he was told that some people cast doubt on the haunting, Cooper smiled and said that he could not vouch for the whole Borley story, but he stuck to his own testimony, even if its first publication contained some inaccuracy.

Some twelve months after interviewing the Coopers, Price spent a day in Sudbury, trying to track down workmen, tradesmen and servants who might have had something to add to the Borley tale. His quest was not very successful; the clues he followed up all seemed to peter out. But he did locate one man, Mr Fred Cartwright, a journeyman carpenter who told him quite a story over a pint of ale at the White Horse.

During the early autumn of 1927 Mr Cartwright lived in lodgings in Sudbury while he was working at some farm buildings between Borley and Clare. Each morning he would walk the shortest way to his work, which chanced to take him past Borley Rectory. On the very first day he passed the place when it was barely light, having left Sudbury soon after six o'clock. Next day he climbed the long hill leading past the Rectory at about the same time (he reckoned it to be about a quarter to seven), and as he passed the drive gate (the one nearest to Sudbury) he saw a Sister of Mercy standing by the gatepost. She looked 'quite normal' but stood very still. Cartwright assumed that she was waiting for someone, and the matter soon passed from his mind. During the next few days he passed the same way at about the same time but he saw no more of the 'Nun' until the following Friday morning when he caught sight of her at exactly the same spot. He thought it rather peculiar for her to be there again at that time of the morning and he looked hard at her as he passed. Once more she appeared to be perfectly normal—except that her eyes were closed. Perhaps, he thought, she had spent the night tending the sick and was resting. He continued on his way.

The following Wednesday at the same time Cartwright again saw the Sister of Mercy at her usual place. As he passed he again looked intently at her and noticed that she looked pale, tired and ill—but otherwise 'perfectly normal'. Again her eyes were closed. This time, after he had walked on, Cartwright felt that something might be wrong and, wondering whether he could help, he turned to offer assistance. But when he reached the place she was nowhere in sight.

The fourth and last time Fred Cartwright saw the 'Nun' was on the following Friday, again at the same spot and the same early hour when it was barely light. As soon as he glimpsed her, he decided to speak—but before he reached the drive, the figure had vanished. 'One moment she had been there, the next she was gone'. Cartwright decided that she must have gone into the Rectory grounds. A little puzzled, he opened the gate and walked the entire length of the drive from one gate to the other, seeing no sign of the figure or anyone inside the building. (His experience occurred between the death of the Reverend Harry Bull and the incumbency of the Reverend G. Eric Smith, so the Rectory was empty.)

When he got home that night, Cartwright spoke of his experiences to his landlord and others at Sudbury. It was then that he heard for the first time the stories and traditions associated with Borley Rectory and the 'phantom nun'. He passed the same way several times during the following years but never saw her again.

Some writers dismissed the journeyman carpenter's account as a 'most interesting story (without dates or corroboration) told to Harry Price three years later' over a pint, with the comment: 'One is inclined to wonder how many more such pints Cartwright had consumed on the strength of it between the appearance of an article on Borley in the national and local press, and when Harry Price sought him out'. This is a somewhat humorous attempt to turn Cartwright into a cadger and a liar—though there is no proof that he was either. Perhaps he may have even paid for his own drinks. And after all, he did relate his experiences to his landlord and others who apparently did not offer such inducements.

Over the years we have made a number of attempts to trace Mr Cartwright, without success, but this is hardly a justification for thinking that he never existed—another surmise which has been put forward by the critics of the hauntings.

During the week that followed his first visit, Price called at the Rectory two or three times. One evening in 1929, when he was accompanied by some friends, 'incessant' bell-ringing occurred, accompanied by the throwing of small pebbles. A shower of keys followed—they appeared to have been collected from various parts of the house and were deposited in the hall, together with 'a small gilt medallion such as Roman Catholic children receive at their Confirmation and another medallion or badge dated 1799 and issued in Paris'.

It has been suggested—though with little force of conviction—that Price lent some 'assistance' to the appearance of the objects, having picked the medals from his numismatic collection. His intention, the accusers said, was to bolster the legend of the Borley hauntings and the ghostly 'Nun'. Strangely enough, Price himself made an error when, in the

text of *'The Most Haunted House in England'*, he referred
to *two* medals being found at Borley in 1929, although he
was correct in referring to *one* medal in the Appendix of
that book and in his notes published in the *Journal* of the
American Society for Psychical Research (of which he was
then foreign research officer), where he mentions the
appearance of 'a brass Romish medallion which the Rector
could not identify' at the same time as the keys and stones
made their appearance. It is worth remembering that Price
was writing *'The Most Haunted House in England'* in difficult conditions after War had been declared and reference to
his original papers was not always easy. There were inaccur-
acies in the 'International Notes' he contributed to the
August 1929 issue of the ASPR's *Journal* (only two months
after his first visit to Borley): statements that the Rectory was
built in 1865 (instead of 1863), that the vaults and cellars
were those of a thirteenth-century monastery and that the
ruins of a nunnery were close by. All these errors Price cor-
rected in his later writings.

Mrs Meeker, Price's secretary who died on 7 May 1955,
asserted firmly that the brass St Ignatius medal (with a Latin
inscription and the head of a monk) was the only medal that
appeared at Borley in the early days and undoubtedly the
only one that appeared on the same night as the six or seven
door-keys. She added that Harry Price was mistaken when he
spoke of *two* medals being found on that occasion in one
part of his first book on the case.

After another visit Price reported what he called an 'impressive' phenomenon. When the visitors and their hosts were
assembled in the Blue Room, someone called for 'a demonstration' and a few moments later one of the bells on the
ground floor rang. Nobody present was able to discover any
explanation. Price said that this 'phenomenon on request' was
repeated at least three times during his investigations at
Borley.

Critics have made much of the fact that objective phenomena of a new kind (throwing of stones, appearance of 'apports' etc) seem to have coincided with Price's first visit to Borley. In addition, it was claimed that poltergeist phenomena and apparitions are rarely, if ever, experienced in the same haunting. But Borley is by no means unique in this respect. Haunted houses in which poltergeist phenomena, apparitions and 'messages' were all experienced include a West Indian case (described in *The Month,* August 1937) and the particularly interesting and well-documented Indian example recounted in the September and October 1929 issues of the same journal. The poltergeist disturbances on Grenada culminated in the burning down of the house. The reported phenomena included mysterious noises and persistent stone-throwing (their weight varying between two ounces and a pound) which drove the occupants out of their home. Eventually, during the night of 14/15 January 1936, the cottage mysteriously caught fire and burned to the ground. Incidents in the Indian case—which, like the Grenadan case, showed distinct similarities to the Borley haunting—including inexplicable outbreaks of fire, movement of objects (including religious medals), locking of doors, displaced and broken kitchen utensils, bricks and other articles thrown, wall-writing, a 'shadow' seen 'high as a human being covered with a black blanket but no human body visible' and a female figure. The household thus affected was that of Mr A. S. Thanghaprogasam Pillay, Deputy-Tahsildar and Sub-Magistrate at the town of Nidamangam, Tanjore, a respected and honourable Catholic, well-known to the bishop and clergy of the district. The Reverend Herbert J. Thurston, who published full details of the case, including much of Mr Pillay's own narrative, in his posthumous *Ghosts and Poltergeists* (London, 1953), went to some trouble to confirm the facts, including consultation with a Salesian missionary who visited the Pillay house several times during the disturbances. Thus Borley can hardly be called unique—and therefore suspect.

In the 1948 *Inky Way Annual* (Book 2) published in December of that year, some nine months after Harry Price's death, Charles Sutton, a veteran reporter of the *Daily Mail*, published a chatty article about his various experiences. This included the following two paragraphs:

> Many things happened the night I spent in the famous Borley Rectory with Harry Price and one of his colleagues, including one uncomfortable moment when a large pebble hit me on the head.
>
> After much noisy 'phenomena' (*sic!*) I seized Harry and found his pockets full of bricks and pebbles. This was one 'phenomenon' he could not explain, so I rushed to the nearest village to phone the *Daily Mail* with my story, but after a conference with the lawyer my story was killed. The News Editor said: 'Bad luck, old man, but there were two of them and only one of you'.

This rather casual and sloppy piece in a popular publication in aid of newspaper charities certainly set the cat among the pigeons. Sutton's charge was gleefully seized upon by Price's quite numerous rivals and enemies; and of course he was not there to defend himself. (Obviously the *Daily Mail* reporter would not have dared to publish these paragraphs if the psychic investigator had been alive, for it would have been promptly followed by a libel suit.) Many thousands of words have been written about Sutton's brief account—the commentaries, analyses, charges and counter-charges monstrously outnumbering the original slender and inexact allegations. Almost every word of it has been placed under a microscope and we can only summarise the main arguments.

The colleague to whom Charles Sutton referred was Miss Lucy Kaye, Price's secretary. The visit itself has been dated by Mr Hastings (not by Sutton, who was vague about it as about so many other things) as having taken place on 25 July 1929. Miss Kaye wrote to the SPR on 21 March 1949, some three months after the publication of the *Inky Way* piece; the following extracts (which Mr Hastings has included in his report) deserve to be quoted in full:

> . . . At the time of the alleged 'exposure' I was working with Mr Price at the Laboratory and also saw something of Sutton from time to time as Mr Price was good enough to invite him to some five sittings with Rudi Schneider—and I must admit that the 'exposure' came as a complete surprise to me . . .
>
> There can be no doubt as to whom Sutton means by Price's 'colleague' at the Rectory, and therefore he attacks my integrity as much as Price's. At Sutton's urgent request I ran him and Price down to Borley that afternoon because Sutton said he was leaving for the U.S.A. over the weekend and it was the last chance he'd get of witnessing the Borley haunt for some months. To our intense disgust Sutton insisted on leaving the Rectory after only about an hour, and required to be given a lift back to the hotel at Long Melford. Price and I decided he was scared, but he insisted he had to phone his story through before midnight if it was to catch the early editions. We pointed out to him that we normally never made the journey from town for so short a vigil, but Sutton was adamant, and with some ill-feeling we returned to the hotel. If my memory serves me well, Sutton did not approach a telephone when we reached the Bull Inn. We had some drinks brought to us in the lounge and sat and chatted amicably for some hours or more. Price took it very well considering the inconvenience we had been put to—as he said next day, 'Funny people these reporters. I never know if its really worth taking them about.' We both felt our evening was wasted.
>
> The question of a 'stone' or 'pebble' must have arisen at some time during the evening (but not, I think, in my presence) for Lord Charles Hope assured me that I appeared to know something about it a few days later but I knew no details, for which I referred him to Price. I HAVE NO MEMORY WHATEVER OF A STONE, BRICK OR PEBBLE EPISODE THAT EVENING, and had there been anything dramatic or sensational like an 'exposure' surely it would have made some impression.
>
> . . . it is my considered conviction that Harry Price never, at any time, faked phenomena. I worked with him in close collabora-

tion for some five years and, indeed, remained friends with him to the day of his death, and I am convinced he was a man of unimpeachable integrity. His urge for publicity was lamented by many, and I am sorry to say is responsible for this *impasse* too. Sutton was the most intelligent of the reporters hanging about for 'news' at the time, and was thrown many tit-bits. He sat with Rudi Schneider five times, witnessing excellent phenomena, and was welcomed at the Laboratory whenever he liked to come in. In fact, I lunched with Sutton in Fleet Street as late as 1940, a thing I would most certainly not have done had there been any of this trouble in the air.

That Miss Kaye genuinely could not recollect the incident Sutton described is shown by a letter she wrote to Price ten years later, on 13 February 1939. Had she remembered the incident, she would surely have mentioned it:

You remember Charles Sutton, who came to Borley with us for the *Mail*? I do not of course know if you are still with him, or not, but on enquiring for him the other [day] I heard that he had an accident about three months ago, when his horse rolled over him, and broke his pelvis. He is just beginning to walk again, and has had a rotten time.

Sutton described in his *Inky Way Annual* piece how he 'rushed' to the nearest phone to report his 'sensational' exposure. As a matter of fact, he was driven to Long Melford by the man whom he was about to denounce in print—and in his company. Would a 'cheat' treat his 'exposer' in such a manner? Would he endure the company of his opponent (or even enemy) a moment longer than necessary?

In the *Annual* article the Borley episode figured only as one of several incidents in Charles Sutton's career as a reporter. But Sutton made various longer and fuller statements —first to Lord Charles Hope who made some notes of these from memory in 1949 (after the *Inky Way* publication) and then to the authors of the SPR Borley report, in 1950. On 6 June 1966, Dr Alan Gauld had an interview with him. There are strong and numerous discrepancies between these various statements which have been examined in detail by Mr Hastings in his March 1969 study of the charges against Harry Price.

As we are not engaged in writing Harry Price's biography nor in presenting an apology for him, we can only concern ourselves with the aspects that are relevant to the Borley story.

It seems to us that the best way of doing this is to present the various versions of the Sutton episode with the appropriate analytical comment. The reader, we believe, can easily make up his mind as to what and whom to believe:

(1) Sutton described how Price, Miss Kaye and himself were about to descend one of three staircases in the Rectory. He heard a slight 'swish' which he thought might be caused by an arm near him and a stone was heard tumbling down the stairs; he thought the time had come to accuse Harry Price (for he says he had had previous suspicions as they visited various rooms in the Rectory); he turned and caught hold of Price, saying: 'Now, I've caught you!' Harry Price said nothing. Sutton asked him to turn his pockets out and, when Price refused, he thrust his hands into both of Price's pockets and brought out several pebbles. Harry Price still said little, hardly defending himself, but kept saying: 'What are you going to do?'

*Lord Charles Hope's notes,* put together about February 1949, after he and Mrs Goldney lunched with Sutton:

Sutton said that he actually saw Price throw the 'stone'.

*Sutton's Testimony given to the* SPR *in* 1950:

. . . As Harry Price was closing the door, however, there was a considerable noise in the room made, so it apeared, by a pebble or stone thrown violently across the room . . . The same 'phenomenon' occurred in all the rooms on the ground floor.

*Sutton, in the interview given to Dr Gauld:*

... I asked him how he was certain that it was a *pebble* which hit his hat as he was lighting the lamp. Did he pick it up and examine it? He replied that he did not find or pick up this or any of the subsequent pebbles which were thrown (except the half-brick on the stairs) and is not now completely certain whether he looked for any of them. He said they 'were not supposed to be' pebbles but to be odd sounds.

(2) Sutton claimed that he 'caught hold of Price', in his 1950 SPR testimony. In a letter to Dr Gauld, dated 14 June 1966, he wrote:

... When I decided that Price might be responsible for throwing the brick, I put the hurricane lamp on the floor and quickly grabbed his coat pockets (*not* his wrist or wrists). When I felt stones, I exclaimed: 'now I have got you,' and thrust my hands into his pockets and felt the stones. I was too quick for Price to resist. He was taken by surprise.

I did *not* seize his wrists. If I had done so, he could have resisted.

(3) In the *Inky Way Annual* Sutton wrote:

'... I seized Harry and found his pockets full of bricks and pebbles ... '

*Dr Gauld's interview:*

' ... I observed that a half-brick would have been a largish object to get into one's pocket; he replied that he thought Price could have had it concealed somewhere about his person ... '

But Sutton did not seem to remember that some seventeen years previously he had spoken not of a half-brick but of *bricks*. Price would have been bulging indeed if he had carried even a single full brick about his person—let alone two or three as Sutton's plural suggested.

(4) Following his telephone conversation with his Editor,

Sutton tells of Price shrugging his shoulders on being told
the result of the reporter's call. On the return journey to
London he was in excellent spirits and even asked whether
Sutton wanted to be present at a future Rudi Schneider
séance.

*Miss Kaye's letter* (21 March 1949):

> . . . If my memory serves me well, Sutton did not approach a
> telephone when we reached the Bull Inn . . .

*Sutton's statement to the* SPR, 1950:

> . . . When I spoke to the *Daily Mail* news editor and then to our
> lawyer I was advised that it would be unwise to write the
> exposure . . .

If this statement means anything, it seems to have involved
at least *three* conversations: first describing the story to the
news editor, then speaking to the lawyer (who must be
assumed to have been available immediately) and finally once
more to the man at the news desk. All this, at a very conser-
vative estimate, must have taken half an hour if not twice as
long. Strangely enough, no critic or investigator thought of
trying to talk to the unnamed news editor or lawyer and
trying to establish whether Mr Sutton made that phone call
at all—or perhaps only imagined it. Now no one except Sutton seems to recall anything.

But the main argument against the truth of Sutton's story
is more valid because it depends not on facts (blurred and
contradictory) but on psychology, the basic make-up of a
man's character. Price was a hot-tempered, impetuous man.
Had Sutton really accused him, he would have reacted with a
punch on the nose rather than some meek muttering. Those
of us who knew him could easily testify that he could and did
lose his temper quickly and gloriously. And Sidney H. Glanville, his friend and neighbour for many years, wrote to Peter
Underwood on 2 September 1950:

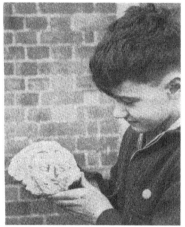

You are perfectly right in your estimate of H.P., he was the last man to sit down under any criticism, especially if he had the slightest idea that it was unjustified—perhaps even if it was! The picture we are given of the incident seems to me to be quite out of character with the man I knew fairly intimately for about thirteen years.

Glanville was quite categoric that, in his personal knowledge, Price's integrity was never open to any doubt—nor had he ever come in contact with or had any knowledge of anybody who had questioned this integrity, prior to the Sutton piece.

But there is a far more powerful argument against the veracity of the *Daily Mail* reporter. Let us suppose that, seeking publicity (of which he had quite a share already), Price decided to produce fake phenomena. Nothing would have been easier for him than to rig up any apparatus he required—the Smiths had vacated the Rectory at least ten days before the Sutton visit—and to stage something far more elaborate and conclusive than dropping a few pebbles or (as Sutton claimed) giving an amateurish performance of ventriloquism. Price was a leading member of the Magic Circle, possessing what was probably one of the most extensive collections of works on conjuring in existence (now part of the Harry Price Library) and was a very clever amateur conjuror. Sidney Glanville said that Price could 'palm a coin like nobody's business', and he sometimes gave conjuring shows for charity. It would have been at least temporary insanity for him to risk the wrecking of his entire career by stuffing his pockets with 'pebbles, stones and bricks' and risk instant exposure by even the most myopic observer.

Mr Hastings sums up the case for Price and against Sutton concisely enough:

(1) Mr Sutton did not *see* Price throwing the stones.
(2) Except in one instance Mr Sutton did not even *see* the stones

he thought had been thrown.

(3) All the phenomena Mr Sutton reported were either *auditory or tactile*; and it is consequently not difficult to think of possible ordinary (non-fraudulent) causes for them.

There is documentary proof that Price continued to make friendly references to Sutton long after the July 1929 incident. It is fruitless to speculate about the motives of those paragraphs in the *Inky Way* or to continue contrasting one person's claims against another, single, testimony. In any case, Price, after some six years' interruption, became closely connected with Borley.

We have discussed Harry Price's experiences with the Foysters. After they left in October 1935, he kept in contact with Borley and received reports about the villagers occasionally seeing a 'strange light' in the Rectory windows. Stories of the sounds of an invisible coach-and-horses frightening the locals also circulated. In February 1936 Price's *Confessions of a Ghost Hunter* was published with some discreet hints that Price had his doubts about the paranormality of the phenomena he witnessed at Borley in 1931 but reaffirming his belief in the genuineness of the earlier experiences he had had there. In March 1936 the Reverend A. C. Henning became Rector but did not take up residence at Borley, living instead at Liston Rectory. Price visited the district on 19 May 1937 and made arrangements to rent the property for a year, paying £30. It was during this visit that he learned, among other things, about the regular motor-coach excursions which were run from Chelmsford, Colchester and Bury St Edmunds during the occupancy of the Smiths 'to see the ghost'.

Price and the new Rector went to have a look at Borley Rectory, after obtaining the keys from Mr and Mrs Arbon, then tenants of the Rectory cottage. They made a careful examination of the house, opening up all the rooms, looking into all the cupboards. The house was completely denuded except for a number of wooden forms and books as, very occasionally, a room had been used for a parish meeting while otherwise the place was kept locked.

Price now faced the problem of how to run his investigation during his tenancy. Rightly or wrongly, he decided to stay out of it himself as far as possible and to keep out his friends and all previous occupants. He wanted to obtain as much independent evidence as he could from 'intelligent, competent and cultured strangers who were not spiritualists'; who, furthermore, would be favoured 'if they knew nothing about psychical research'. He inserted an advertisement in *The Times* of 25 May 1937, asking for responsible persons of leisure and intelligence, intrepid, critical and unbiased, to join a rota of observers. The response was immediate and overwhelming; over two hundred applications were received. Price sorted out about a quarter of them as being worth serious consideration and in due course selected about forty people, all total strangers to him, after a personal interview with each of them. He prepared a 'Blue Book of Instructions'; each observer was required to sign a declaration agreeing to carry out these instructions, to pay his own expenses, not to disclose the name or locality of the house, not to write or cause to be written any account of his experiences, not to take any unauthorised person there, not to take any photograph or make sketches without written permission, to furnish a report of each observational period, to lock all doors and windows on leaving and to deposit the keys as directed. The applicant was also required not to be connected with the press in any way. The 'Blue Book' also told the inexperienced observers what to do if bell-ringing, footsteps or other noises were heard or apparitions seen, where to get a meal, and other pertinent information.

His critics suggested that it would have been wiser if Price had sought the help of people with some experience in psychical research. He did not do so, they said, because his object was simply to obtain information for a 'good story'. He kept the experts away, they added, lest they should spoil his project. And the 'Blue Book' would implant in the minds of the inexperienced laymen suggestions as to what they might see, hear and feel—so that they were more likely to report the occurrence of such phenomena.

The SPR has complained that it did not have the opportunity of investigating these alleged phenomena, but, as we have already pointed out, it had information about Borley before Harry Price did and, of course, once press publicity began, it was in no way prevented from approaching the incumbents. Finally, it was perfectly free to rent or buy the Rectory after Price's tenancy expired. It did none of these things.

Price picked the study or library as a Base Room. It was furnished with a camp bed, a paraffin table-lamp, a spirit kettle, cutlery, a supply of tea, sugar and other basic necessities. Twenty books—none of them on psychical research—were provided to help fill the long hours.

On 2 June 1937, Harry Price and an Oxford graduate friend, Mr Ellic Howe, drove to Borley, set up the Base Room and then made a careful examination of the Rectory.

During their tour they 'ringed' with coloured chalk every movable object and placed a few small things here and there, also carefully 'ringing' them. They discovered a lady's dirty and rather moth-eaten blue serge coat hanging on the door of the Blue Room. It had not been there when Price had examined the Rectory with Mr Henning a fortnight earlier—and though he made numerous enquiries he could not discover how it came to be there. According to Price, one observer reported that the coat disappeared completely for one week—and then reappeared.

After visiting Mr and Mrs Payne at Borley Place, opposite the Rectory, they examined the grounds and then decided to stay the night. At about nine pm while they were in the Base

Room, they heard a series of short sharp taps in quick succession, emanating apparently from the passage just outside. They explored, but found nothing to account for the taps; all the doors were as they had been left and nothing unusual was seen. Fifteen minutes later they were disturbed by two loud 'thumps', followed by the noise of a door being slammed, apparently upstairs. Again, nothing whatever appeared to have been moved or disturbed; both exterior and interior doors were exactly as they had been left. They also searched the grounds. About an hour later, since it had turned chilly and there was no way of heating the Base Room, Price and Howe decided to return to London. First they saw Mr and Mrs Arbon, who had been tenants of the cottage since February 1936, and arranged for them to take charge of one set of keys. They were told that Price would either advise them of the arrival of an observer or arrange for the latter to present a letter of introduction. Under no circumstances were the keys to be handed to any unauthorised person. The Arbons agreed to observe these precautions.

Some twenty-two years later, on 19 August 1959, we met Mr Howe and he told again the story of that first visit to Borley with Price. He stated that there was undoubted movement of small objects which Price could not have caused. There were other incidents in the Blue Room and elsewhere. Mr Howe knew Price well and he considered it out of the question that the psychic investigator should have put on such a show for his benefit—even if it had been possible for him to do so.

Mr Sidney H. Glanville and his son were the first to do duty as observers at the Rectory; they subsequently spent many hours there both in the daytime and at night during Price's tenancy. They reported a number of unexplained noises, including thuds and footsteps, further pencil markings and the pendule-like movement of a window blind. Mr Mark Kerr-Pearse, later British Pro-Consul at Basra, also spent much time at the Rectory. He heard many raps, thumps, thuds and other sounds for which no explanation was ever discovered; he reported the movement of 'controlled' objects, among them a bag of coal weighing fifty pounds. He, too, discovered a number of new pencil markings, a lump of rotten touchwood and a mummified frog. Once, after entering a room, he heard a click and found himself locked in.

On 16 July 1937, the first attempt at table-rapping took place at Borley. Mr Kerr-Pearse reported that he sat in the Base Room with Mr and Mrs Henning and soon after 9.30 pm began their experiment. After about the fourth attempt, a 'most extraordinary noise' was heard apparently emanating from the kitchen and moving slowly down the passage towards the three occupants of the Rectory. It lasted a full minute but ceased abruptly when the three people stood up to get a better view of the passage. They were quite unable to find any reason for the noise; the Hennings told us later that they had never obtained a satisfactory explanation of this curious and disturbing experience.

Other observers included Mr Rupert Haig, Mr Kerr-Pearse's cousin who, while resting in the Base Room, was awakened by an icy draught playing on his face. At the time all the doors and windows were closed, a big fire was burning in the fireplace and the temperature was 60° F.

Colonel Westland discovered a piece of wood on the stairs and a round blue box containing pins which had not been reported before; later this was found to have moved half an inch out of the chalked circle.

Dr H. F. Bellamy made an electric bell contact-breaker and placed it under a pile of books on the dining-room mantelpiece. When the bell rang it was seen that all the books had been displaced and the bottom one was pushed right off the contact-breaker. Once one of Dr Bellamy's friends felt his hair ruffled in the dark while another had his face touched.

The list of observers was a long one. There was Mr S. J.

de Lotbinière, head of the BBC's Outside Broadcasts Department, who heard 'clicks' and a 'scrabbling' noise; Major H.
Douglas-Home; Mr John Snagge; Mr W. S. Hammond; Mr
C. S. Taylor; Mr G. J. Bell; Mr J. Thurley; Mr C. Gordon
Glover and Mr Lloyd Williams (a director of the BBC's Edu-
cational Department) with their wives; and Mr M. Savage, a
television engineer. Graduates and undergraduates included
Messrs J. M. Bailey and C. V. Wintour, who thought they saw
the letter 'M' grow in front of their eyes; Mr S. G. Welles who
reported a luminous patch of light on the ceiling of the Blue
Room; Mr J. Burden and Mr T. Stainton who heard shuffling
footsteps, the noise of swishing garments, a 'dragging noise',
and a continuous wailing sound coming from the Blue Room,
and who found fresh pencil markings. Still other observers
were Mr R. Hawkin, Mr R. J. Milberg and Mr M. P. Knox;
Dr C. E. M. Joad spent an observational period at the Rectory and, after carefully noting all marks on the white-washed
walls, was 'reasonably certain' that another pencil squiggle
had appeared an hour later. The late Commander A. B.
Campbell RN, also of the BBC Brains Trust, shared a common
interest in occult matters with Joad who discussed with him
his Borley visit and told his fellow-panellist that he received
a blow on the cheek from a piece of soap in a sealed room.
Discussing this incident at a meeting of the Ghost Club in
December 1960, Commander Campbell added that Joad had
placed a thermometer on the mantelpiece in the same closed
and sealed room—which showed a sudden drop of ten degrees.
(It is, of course, an established fact that temperatures drop
during séance-room phenomena.) While the soap incident
might have been due to human agency, it is difficult to see
how the temperature of a sealed room, containing four people
all night, could show such a reading.

Flight-Lieutenant R. Carter Jonas (later Air Commodore
Jonas, CBE) and Flight-Lieutenant Caunter described finding
a nail-file in the pantry; they spent the night at the Rectory

and while they did *not* hear any of the creaks and noises usually audible in most houses during the hours of darkness, on a different visit noticed an 'overwhelming' smell of incense. Mr F. A. Mansbridge of the Bank of England was at Borley with his wife who felt her coat belt being lifted and dropped. Mr A. P. Drinkwater of Longmans Green, the publishers, and three friends heard percussive knocks and a heavy thump from the direction of the Blue Room, found the blue box that had (seemingly) moved yet again from its chalk ring and discovered many new pencil markings. Dr and Mrs Joseph reported curious noises; they described the house as 'repellent' and remarked on the absolute, oppressive silence. Mrs Lloyd Williams thought she saw a round, stooping figure in the Rectory garden that could have been the 'Nun'.

Price's twelve-month tenancy ended on 19 May 1938 and he went to Borley with a neighbour, Mr Geoffrey H. Motion, to collect his belongings, tidy up the place and hand the keys back to Mr Henning. It was his first visit for many weeks. He and his companion walked round the garden, carefully examined every room and cupboard, collected the odds and ends scattered through the house and deposited them in the Base Room. After taking some refreshment, they made another tour of the house, examining all rooms, cupboards, walls and floors. So complete was their scrutiny that a single matchstick (duly enclosed in its chalk circle) was found on the floor of the Blue Room. The cellars were also examined. At about half-past six Price and Motion went to Sudbury after carefully locking the Rectory. Returning about an hour later, they found everything normal, had a word with the Arbons and learned that efforts were being made again to sell the Rectory. At 8 pm another complete round of the tour was made to see whether anything had happened while they were away. Everything was as they had left it. They packed the camp-bed, stove and all the other bits and pieces into Mr

Motion's car and at 10 pm made another uneventful tour of the house. Just before midnight yet another circuit of the house was carried out and this time, as they entered the Blue Room, their torches immediately focused on a 22-carat gold wedding ring, shining in the opening between the Blue Room and the adjoining dressing-room. Later Price discovered that the ring was an ordinary wedding ring, not very much worn and made in Birmingham in 1864—the year after the Rectory was first occupied. No one ever claimed it. Price recalled the wedding ring that was found in the bathroom on 10 March 1931 during the Foyster occupancy. Next morning it had disappeared. He added that the ring he and Mr Motion discovered may have found its way into the Rectory in a perfectly normal manner; though it seems unlikely that if it had been there, he and his companion would not have seen it during their previous tours. Another minute search followed for other possible 'apports', but nothing was found.

Price's critics blamed him for making no attempt to direct the investigation, keeping no log book and leaving each group of observers to carry out an enquiry without previous experience. They suggested, as we have mentioned before, that the sounds of footsteps were either hallucinatory or belonged to actual, living people outside the Rectory. They referred to Major Douglas-Home's statement that Mr and Mrs Arbon used to work the handpump in the courtyard very late at night 'causing groans and thumps galore' and that the Arbons' footsteps were clearly audible in each room of the house, which is an interesting, if exaggerated, suggestion. As to the curious door-locking incident of Mr Mark Kerr-Pearse, they suggested that he locked the door automatically himself as he entered. The Harry Price tenancy was summed up by the authors of the SPR report as providing such slender evidence for any paranormal activity during the period as to be worthless—a statement with which, of course, many of the observers themselves would disagree.

Mr S. H. Glanville left the original copy of his *Locked Book* to the 'disarming and persuasive' Trevor H. Hall, one of the three authors of the SPR report. Harry Price's close friend Sidney Glanville was always very careful to ensure the secrecy of information given to him in confidence, and parts of the *Locked Book* are clearly headed 'private and confidential' or 'strictly confidential'. In spite of this, a good deal of this private and confidential material was published in an article by Trevor H. Hall and his daughter Kathryn which appeared in the *International Journal of Parapsychology* (Summer 1959). The motive for disregarding Glanville's wishes was given as trying to illustrate how séance messages about matters known to the sitters can be influenced by suggestion. Yet there was at least an underlying additional effect: to criticise and belittle Sidney Glanville and his friends.

In his published accounts of the Borley haunting, Price examined the wall-writings and messages and relates details of the table-tipping and planchette sessions carried out at Borley and elsewhere. It should be sufficient to explain here that the general theme of most of the information received referred to a nun named Marie Lairre. Sister Lairre had come to England from France in the seventeenth century, the planchette 'revealed', had been murdered and wanted mass and prayers said for her at Borley Rectory.

One planchette sitting, however, held on 27 March 1938, deserves special mention. On this occasion Miss Helen Glanville, daughter of Price's collaborator, tried this method of communication as she had done previously in October 1937. (Helen Glanville later married a Mr Carter.) In his *Locked Book* Glanville relates (as he told us personally) that he had bought a planchette board some years before going to Borley; but though he tried to carry out some experiments, the board had persistently refused to move or produce any writing— until it was taken to Borley. On 27 March 1938, Helen Glanville and her brother Roger obtained a message from an entity calling itself 'Sunex Amures', stating that the Rectory would be burnt down at nine o'clock that night, that bones and 'proof of the haunting' would be found under the ruins and that the fire would start over the hall. Nothing happened that night—but, exactly eleven months later, at midnight on 27 February 1939, the Rectory was gutted by fire when a lamp was upset in the hall.

Most serious psychical researchers would agree that any information obtained at séances must not be taken too seriously or too literally. Our own experience of this type has not been altogether convincing; we have received information we had *not* thought to be within the normal knowledge of anyone but ourselves—but we have also been told a vast amount of nonsense. On rare occasions, many people believe, it is possible that communication with some discarnate entity may be established—but much more rarely than generally claimed. As for the Borley séances, they must be treated with great reserve. We include reports of some of them only because they form an integral part of the story and must be taken into account—but it is necessary to keep a tight hold on one's imagination in assessing the value of such communications.

Following a broadcast on the Borley haunting (during which Borley Rectory was not mentioned by name) Harry Price received a letter from Captain W. H. Gregson informing him that he had bought the Rectory. (The purchase took place in December 1938.) Price asked for details of any inexplicable incidents for possible inclusion in the book he was planning. Captain Gregson responded by describing what happened when he was showing the Rectory to one of the many strangers who flocked to Borley hoping to 'see the ghost'. In the library (the old Base Room) the visitor suddenly became very ill—because, he said, of the 'malevolent influence' he felt. Captain Gregson added that he felt nothing himself—but he 'liked to think that there was really something eerie as it added charm to the place ... '

At the time of the fire, Captain Gregson and his sons Alan and Andrew had been living at the cottage, planning to move to the Rectory a little later. The new owner was sorting books in the hall when a lamp overturned; within a few minutes the flames had spread and the fire became out of control.

During Gregson's ownership one or two curious things happened. These included the unexplained removal of a heavy hatch-cover made for the well in the cellar; the breaking of a drinking glass and the disappearance of the water it contained; the sound of footsteps in the courtyard which apparently terrified the family's cocker spaniel, which began to howl and rushed out of the Rectory grounds; unexplained footsteps which seemed to originate from the kitchen part; and numerous small objects being moved or upset. During a broadcast in the BBC series 'In Town Tonight' on 15 April 1939, Captain Gregson related the story of the terrified dog which never returned; he bought another spaniel puppy which behaved exactly like its predecessor one day—and was never seen again. However, Peter Underwood was told by Mrs Henning that the day after the first dog had run off, it was seen in Borley village, apparently having a fit, and was shot. The second dog, according to some reports, was run over by a car and killed.

After the fire which destroyed the Rectory in February 1939, two other mysterious figures were reported. A police constable questioned Captain Gregson about a 'woman in grey and a man wearing a bowler hat', apparently 'cloaked', who were seen coming out of the Rectory while the fire was raging. The captain replied that there had been no one in the house at the time of the outbreak except himself. Yet another unexplained figure, looking like a young girl, was seen by several local people at an upper window of the blazing Rectory. It may have been the same figure that suddenly appeared at the opening of the burnt-out window of the Blue Room and was seen, on the night of 26 March 1939, by Mr

Charles Graham Browne of Pound Hall, Melford, and Miss Rosemary M. Williams, daughter of Captain Williams of Borley Lodge, near Sudbury. They watched it for several seconds before it vanished. Miss Williams thought the girl was dressed in light blue and was struck by the natural and attractive appearance of the figure—even though it stood at a spot where, in the burnt-out shell of the building, no one could have been expected to linger. The report she made is preserved in Price's Borley file. Contrary to what some critics said, he did not pay for it (thereby perhaps weakening its authenticity); though Miss Williams originally asked for the modest fee of a guinea to provide a statement, Price refused to pay because, as he rightly pointed out, any report obtained in such a way would be worthless.

On 16 March 1939, less than three weeks after the fire, Mr Herbert Mayes, former chauffeur to the Reverend A. C. Henning, happened to be cycling past the ruins one dark and moonless night on his way home. When he passed the Rectory grounds, he heard the sound of approaching horses, travelling at great speed. (Mr Mayes gave his account to Peter Underwood; he died in 1951.) Similar sounds had been heard many years earlier by the Reverend Harry Bull. Mayes thought that some of the horses at Borley Place must have broken loose and were stampeding. He jumped off his bicycle and stood close to the hedge on the side of the road, turning his cycle lamp in the direction of the approaching sounds. The galloping hooves appeared to come nearer, passed him and finally died away in the distance—but he saw nothing that could have accounted for the sounds. The noise of horses' hooves was heard again from the direction of the Rectory site in 1953 by five members of the party taken to the burnt-out house by Dr A. J. B. Robertson, MA, PHD, a former council member of the SPR. This was during a series of visits by students which became known as the investigation of the Cambridge Commission.

Price visited Borley on 21 June 1939 when a 'Psychic Fête' was held in the Rectory grounds, attended by a number of members of the old Ghost Club. It was organised by Mr Henning and his church council to raise funds for the restoration of Borley church and was opened by the late Mrs R. A. Butler, wife of the future Chancellor of the Exchequer and Master of Trinity.

In August 1940 Price's *'The Most Haunted House in England'* was published. At its conclusion he said that his readers were then in possession of all the evidence he had gathered about the alleged haunting—but it was for them to decide whether the place was haunted or not. He went on to ask whether phenomena observed at Borley Rectory could be explained in terms of our known physical laws, whether all the hundred-odd witnesses were mad, liars or victims of hallucination once they had crossed the 'enchanted boundary' of Borley village. In his own opinion the answer to all these questions was 'no'—and he ended by affirming his belief in the authenticity of the Borley haunting. The final verdict he left to his readers.

One of these readers was W. J. Phythian-Adams, Canon of Carlisle, who read Price's book over the Christmas holiday. He was sufficiently interested in the story to write to Harry Price in January 1941, offering a brilliant analysis of the whole of the Borley haunting, based on new interpretations of the wall-writings, séance messages and evidence presented in Price's work. His hypothesis certainly accounted for practically all the alleged paranormal phenomena at Borley, including a plausible and reasonable explanation for the happenings. The most outstanding point referred to the fact that most of the messages and many other 'pointers' suggested human remains waiting to be found under the cellar floor.

Price himself admitted freely that, had it not been for the canon's 'analytical essays' (which actually resulted in the discovery of such human remains in the place he suggested), he would probably never have attempted his second book on the Borley case. We shall deal with the excavations in our next chapter; here it should be sufficient to say that Mr Leslie J. Godden, a West End dental surgeon (with whom Peter Underwood discussed this particular aspect at a Ghost Club meeting in 1958), identified the human bones as having probably belonged to a young woman. She had suffered, as Mr Godden stated, from a deep-seated abscess which must have caused much pain—and could have accounted for the fact that whenever the 'Nun' was seen, she was invariably described as 'pale-faced', 'sad', with 'drawn face' or 'looking as if she had been crying'. (Not a very romantic explanation, but a reasonably realistic one.) The bones were duly buried in Liston churchyard on 29 May 1945 by Mr Henning, in the presence of Mrs Henning, young Stephen Henning and Price.

Price gave a number of reasons for delaying his excavations at Borley following Canon Phythian-Adams's suggestion to test his theories. In 1941 he was not in possession of many clues, pointers and indications which he later acquired. Nor was there any urgency about the matter; the lower portion of the Rectory was still standing and no hint had reached him that it might be demolished. Captain Gregson was trying to sell the grounds and the shell of the Rectory and would not have welcomed further damage to the property. Nor was East Anglia a particularly healthy spot in 1941 when German air attacks were particularly concentrated. Once Mr Henning was nearly blown out of his car as he drove up to his Rectory and bombs exploded in a circle around his home. To hire labour for the excavation of the cellars and walls would have been particularly difficult at this period. Price himself was busy with other chores. His home was nearly a hundred and fifty miles from Borley and he did not like to spend a night away from home if he could help it. All these factors provided reasons for his visiting Borley rarely during his tenancy and the following years.

However, on 17 August 1943, after an unsuccessful search for the entrance to the church crypt, digging took place in the cellars of the ruined Rectory and continued for two days. We deal in detail with this eventful operation in our next chapter. The cellar was completely emptied; a fine Sheffield plate cream jug was found, together with various odds and ends, such as broken tiles, potsherds and empty bottles. The cellar floor was breached and human bones and two religious medals or pendants discovered. Those present at the digging included the Reverend and Mrs A. C. Henning, Mrs Alexander English (formerly Miss E. Beenham), Mrs Georgina Dawson and Captain Gregson.

The critics of Price elaborated in their report the fact that Mr Glanville was absent from the diggings and that in his view the planchette material originated in the subconscious mind of its operators. He never believed, they add, that such a person as Marie Lairre ever existed; nor did he accept the alleged 'apports' although he was convinced that during the observation periods of himself, his son and a small group of friends (for whose integrity and critical faculty he could vouch personally) a number of inexplicable incidents, mostly auditory, occurred under good conditions. Certainly, Glanville's accounts of some of these happenings provide one of the most puzzling factors of the whole case. Glanville had to insist— and he told us, quite firmly—that these statements should appear in the SPR book.

Was it so curious that Price did not invite his neighbour and friend Glanville to the excavations? Was there some ulterior motive behind this omission? In fact, after the compilation of his *Locked Book*, covering his association with Borley from the date in 1937 when he approached Price to become an official observer until the Psychic Fête in 1939, Glanville's part in the investigation diminished considerably. Though he followed the case with some interest, once he had completed his *Locked Book* he made no major contribution

to the Borley case. Glanville, though a friend and neighbour of Price, never regarded himself as his special associate and confidant in psychical research—not even on the Borley case. Throughout the *Locked Book* the numerous letters exchanged by the two men remained on the formal plane—addressing one another as 'Dear Mr Glanville' and 'Dear Mr Price'. Mr R. F. Aickman (with whom Peter Underwood has discussed Borley and its problems on several occasions) contributed an article called 'Postscript to Harry Price' to the *London Mystery Magazine* of August/September 1950 in which he remarked that although he was in close communication with Price when he (Mr Aickman) and his friends made the visits to Borley recorded in *The End of Borley Rectory*, Price said nothing about visiting the place almost immediately before and after their visits in order to carry out the excavations. Mrs Henning, writing to Mrs C. C. Baines on 3 February 1957, added another aspect to the reason for Glanville's absence, protesting against the SPR critics' view of 'Mr Glanville's not being there as calculated treachery'. She explained: 'I had only two spare rooms then—the Bull at Long Melford was full of officers and their wives . . . '

Talking about the possibility of something more 'than mere inexact reporting' in the discovery of the bone fragments by Harry Price, the critics suggest that he deliberately failed to invite Glanville to Borley—so as not to be embarrassed by a witness whose absolute integrity no one has ever questioned. They added that the fact that the bone fragments were found only three feet down, or only inches below the bottom of the original trough, made nonsense of the claim of their being remains of a body dropped into the well which was afterwards filled in. The closeness of these fragments to the surface, they continued, could easily lead to the suspicion that they were placed there deliberately—by someone who was anxious to do the least possible work to 'prove' a theory quickly and without trouble. As for the two oval pendants, the opponents of Price hint—though without adducing any proof—that they may have come from Price's numismatic collection. They did not offer any explanation as to the condition of the pendants—verified by the participants of the 1943 diggings which included (in addition to those already mentioned) Dr E. H. Bailey, Mr Roland F. Bailey (a barrister), Flying-Officer A. A. Creamer and a Mr Jackson, a local resident. There was a thick coating of clay and patina that had to be removed before they were identified and they had to be scrubbed before traces of figures and letters could be distinguished. It would be extremely difficult if not impossible to 'fake' such incrustations. Incidentally, religious medals have been dug up elsewhere in the district, including Long Melford, a mile or so from Borley. Those present agreed that the flooring of the Rectory cellars had not been disturbed for many years. To place objects at a depth of three feet without leaving traces would have been quite an achievement—and for Harry Price to plan and carry out such a planting of evidence would have entailed considerable precognition; for how could he have known, in advance, of Canon Phythian-Adams's suggestion to dig under the 'well-tank', a suggestion based on the canon's interpretation of the wall-messages? Price, even if he had been endowed with such clairvoyant powers, would have run considerable risk in carrying out such complex and lengthy 'preparations' in a place that was under fairly regular observation by the Cambridge Commission and others—not to mention the locals.

The same decisive argument applies to the bone fragments. Human remains have been dug up at Bures, a few miles from Borley, at a depth of 'about four feet' in 1947, as the *Suffolk and Essex Free Press* reported on 7 August of that year.

Though Mr Kerr-Pearse as early as July 1937 had suggested looking '*in* the well', Price did not react to this advice. In a letter to S. H. Glanville on 20 July 1937, he referred casually to the suggestion but took no action until Canon Phythian-

Adams's analysis provided a more acceptable reason for digging. (Of course, the fact that the Rectory had burned down in the meantime made excavations easier than in an intact building, even if temporarily uninhabited.) If he had wanted to 'plant' evidence earlier, he certainly could have done so.

There is another, even stronger, argument against Harry Price being involved in any skulduggery about human bones. He was a devout churchgoer and sidesman at his local church at Pulborough where the rector always spoke of him as 'a man of complete integrity'. It has been pointed out that a practising member of the Church of England would hardly be likely to arrange Christian burial for the remains of the alleged 'Marie Lairre', with the last rites being given to whatever was left of her bones, if he had rigged the whole affair. Psychologically and physically the evidence against anything like this happening must be accepted as quite conclusive.

There were a number of incidents in the history of the Borley haunting that must be mentioned here. In 1942 a Mr Samuel Seal of Bures, stationed as an army sergeant on a searchlight battery at Belchamp Walter, happened to pass the Rectory site late one night on his way to the camp. Half-way up the hill leading to the burnt-out building and Borley church, he saw two lights coming towards him very fast. He thought it must be a private car, but when about a hundred yards from him, the lights switched across the road and disappeared. Mr Seal noticed a dark shape following them. He thought that the vehicle had gone through the gates of the old Rectory, but when he reached the spot where the 'phantom' had vanished, he found the gate was closed. In 1945 Mr Seal told us that only after he described his experiences to some friends did he learn about the haunting associated with Borley Rectory.

Some two years later, in July 1944, Lieutenant Aitchison, while visiting Mr Glanville at Fittleworth, undertook a psy-

chometric experiment with the objects found at Borley. When
he handled the French Revolution medal, he 'saw' an 'old
man, bent, something wrong with his right leg'; while the
nail-file found by two of Price's observers produced the reaction that it had been taken from a person who had been
murdered, probably drowned. With the 'Miraculous Medal'
(details of which are given in our next chapter), Lieutenant
Aitchison felt that a young girl was involved; that she was
wearing the medal and that there was something very tight
around her waist. Handling the child's Roman Catholic confirmation medal provoked the comment: 'I have only a
troubled, frightened feeling from it'; while the thin gold pendant really upset the psychometrist. He felt that its owner had
wanted to get rid of it, that it had been worn round the neck
of a girl and had been torn off. He also 'saw' a small room
with boards forming a bed at one side, then he felt the wearer
was lying on the boards with someone on top of her and when
she felt the medal she pulled it off and threw it away. He
added: 'Very trying time'. The jawbone gave the opposite
impression to Lieutenant Aitchison: 'Florence, happiness'
and the feeling that the owner was doubtful about following
a suggestion to start another place on her own; that 'it wasn't
strangulation but rape, that Waldegrave did it' . . . and a
'feeling of shame'. Holding both the jawbone and the skull
fragment, the experimenter felt that the rest of the remains
should be found and buried properly, some distance from the
Rectory. When he handled the wedding ring found by Harry
Price and G. H. Motion in 1938, he shouted: 'Murder!'
dropped the ring and refused to touch it again.

The origin of the bone fragments is unlikely ever to be
established satisfactorily. We agree with those who regretted
their burial, since in recent years great strides have been made
in dating such remains and today it would be possible to de-
termine their age far more reliably and definitely than it was
at the time of the burial some thirty years ago. Nor did the

burial appear to have placated the unquiet spirit at Borley Rectory.

The coroner for the district was informed at the time of the discovery of the human remains and agreed with Harry Price that they were too small to warrant an inquest. (This was disclosed by Price in a lecture he gave at Sudbury, Suffolk, in 1947, to help raise funds for restoring the pre-Reformation altar at Borley church.)

In December 1942 Mr Guy P. J. L'Estrange, formerly of Bungay, Suffolk, a former medium and member of the Marks Tey Spiritualist Circle, published an article in the *Norwich Mercury*, describing a visit he said he made to the Rectory during the Foyster incumbency. The rector, L'Estrange wrote, told him of 'unearthly forms', flickering lights, mysterious footsteps, of whispering and other noises, of the unexplained writings—even of seeing a pencil one day rise from his desk and scrawl words on the wall. L'Estrange himself claimed to have witnessed bottles appearing suddenly in mid-air and smashing to pieces, spontaneous bell-ringing, footsteps and seeing an 'indistinct figure'.

L'Estrange, a Justice of the Peace and a local figure of some standing, was strongly attacked by critics of the Borley case. They did this without interviewing him and subsequently had to print an apology. Yet L'Estrange reaffirmed that he had had paranormal experiences at Borley Rectory and recounted his story to Peter Underwood in the presence of Mr S. F. C. Kiernander. Apart from this, Price received many reports of curious happenings in the vicinity of the place, especially after the publication of his first Borley book—some of which he published in *The End of Borley Rectory*, which appeared in 1946. Some of these are well worth repeating here as examples of the variety of phenomena and to show the type of person who was visiting the site and sending Price reports.

Mr H. F. Russell, acting chairman and manager of a famous cable company, described a visit he made to Borley

with his two sons—one of them a wing-commander and the
other a squadron-leader—on 12 November 1941. His sons had
entered the house when Mr Russell, some twenty yards behind them, felt himself suddenly seized and dashed to the
ground where he landed in a pool of mud.

During the wartime blackout, in the period after the Rectory had been burnt down, Mrs Savage, who lived nearby,
claimed that lights were often seen in the ruins and the ARP
authorities investigated the mystery more than once.

Three Polish officers, attached to the Army Medical Corps
of the Polish forces, paid two visits to Borley, on 28-29 June
and 28-29 July 1943. On the second occasion two officers and
two English boys were present. They reported a striking
variety of spectacular incidents to which they ascribed paranormal causes. At this time the Rectory was a completely gutted ruin. Existing doors opened and closed unaccountably;
there were 'whisperings', curious noises of various kinds, inexplicable shadows and black shapes—on no less than six
occasions stones were thrown. These reports were disparaged
and completely dismissed by the critics; but the Polish officers
were neither impressionable youths nor newspapermen seeking to distort evidence for the sake of sensationalism; they had
no axe to grind and it would be difficult to suggest any motive
for supplying untrue reports to Price, whom they did not
know. The officers included the CO of the unit and Lieutenant Nawrocki, a doctor of medicine who had shown an interest in scientific psychical research for many years.

Three days later an entirely different party visited the
ruins and also reported stone-throwing. A pebble struck Miss
George, a friend of Mr and Mrs Aickman, who visited the
ruins accompanied by Mr L. W. J. Jelinek on 1 August 1943.

Two undergraduates from Trinity College, Oxford, reported a couple of minor but curious incidents—and, more
puzzling, an unexplained voice—on a visit on 5 January 1944.
One of them, Mr J. H. Russell, was walking through the old

orchard away from the house when he heard his friend, Mr Harry Marshall, call him by name. The latter was standing on the cart-track running through the orchard, about fifteen yards in front of Mr Russell. Mr Marshall had, in fact, *not* called at all.

In December 1941 Surgeon-Lieutenant R. R. Prewer, RNVR, notified Price that the army were trying to use the ruined Rectory and that they were 'troubled by poltergeist activity'.

At this period Mr Robert Fordyce Aickman (a long-standing member of the Ghost Club) visited Borley a number of times with friends. One report sent to Price by him stated that the military authorities had demolished the pseudo-Gothic summer-house and had dug in the garden. The Reverend A. C. Henning later wrote to Price reporting that an officer and some men arrived at the Rectory one night determind to sleep there, but the men refused to enter as they did not like the look of the place. The officer, who knew nothing of the place's reputation, ultimately slept there alone and was awakened several times during the night by the sound of ringing bells.

In August 1943 Price published an article in *Everybody's Weekly* which led to a number of letters reaching him and the editor. Two of these were reproduced in *The End of Borley Rectory*. The first came from the much-travelled and well-known film comedian, Gilbert Hayes. Mr Hayes had been looking for a suitable place to turn into a tea-garden and visited Borley Rectory as a possible site in September 1939. At that time *'The Most Haunted House in England'* had not been published. Mr Hayes did not know Price and had never heard of the haunting; he visited Borley with his wife and heard footsteps which followed him as he explored the house. He also heard the noise of a door closing. Some grocery receipts appeared to have been 'inexplicably moved', and later footsteps were again heard.

A Mr A. S. Medcraft of Goodmayes, Essex, wrote to Price on 27 April 1943 about a visit he paid to Borley early one July, a day of brilliant sunshine. Within two hundred yards of the Rectory he heard footsteps following him. When he stopped and turned round, the footsteps ceased and the road was empty. When he resumed walking towards the Rectory the footsteps again seemed to follow him but this time appeared to be slower than his own. Suddenly he turned his head. The footsteps ceased as before—again he found himself looking at the empty road. Reaching the summer-house, he sat down on the lawn, facing the Rectory, to eat some sandwiches. Everything was quiet but about half an hour later he heard a tremendous bang—as if a door had slammed. He investigated immediately, but all was still as before. There was no wind. While passing the french windows, he noticed a peculiar and strong but quite pleasant smell which he could not account for as there was nothing around in the way of flowers or plants that could have produced it.

Between 1939 and 1944, a number of students, mostly from St John's College, Cambridge, visited Borley under the leadership of Dr Andrew J. B. Robertson. These visits became known as the Cambridge Commission and a meticulously detailed report was eventually issued. Fifty-eight people spent one night or more at the ruined Rectory during twenty-five visits. In November 1944 Dr Robertson read a paper at a meeting of the SPR and explained that in general the approach of these observers to the haunting was one of comparative scepticism. By 1944 something like one-third of the investigators had reported nothing out of the ordinary, about another third described incidents which they thought 'might not be expected to occur in the normal way', and the remaining third described events which seemed to them 'definitely unusual'. Among these, peculiar noises were the most common; they included footsteps, knocks, taps, hammerings, thuds, bangs, cracks, rumblings, the stamping of horses' hooves and whistles. There were some curious temperature changes, two cases of markings appearing in pencil on paper and one of the displacement of an object. On the final visit of the five-year investigation a party of students arrived and attempted to fake some 'ghostly phenomena'. But they were quickly detected by the official observers and their rather childish prank was frustrated.

Critics of the Borley case remarked that although Dr Robertson organised the visits, he was present on only eight occasions out of twenty-five. As far as the auditory phenomena were concerned, they claimed these were due to the ruins gradually disintegrating and later being demolished. Yet Dr Robertson emphasised that it was very unusual for any noise to be noted when the observers were moving about in the ruins. There were also some mysterious lights seen by two of them.

In 1944 Harry Price visited Borley accompanied by Miss Cynthia Ledsham and Mr David E. Scherman during which several 'flying bricks' were observed. Miss Ledsham was said to have told the London SPR that there was a man still at work behind the wall—which, of course, would have explained the mysterious occurrences. She added that all three visitors saw the workman and that there could be no doubt about his being responsible for the 'flying bricks'. Mr Scherman, the *Life* photographer who took a much-reproduced picture of one of these 'missiles', corroborated Miss Ledsham's account of the incident; in fact, a workman was plainly visible on the extreme left of the photograph Price published in *The End of Borley Rectory*. While Price presented the event as a possibly paranormal phenomenon, he was careful *not* to state that no workmen were there at the time. Indeed, it would have been impossible for him not to be aware of their presence. He said: 'demolition was in progress' and went on: 'no workmen were present on that side of the ruins'—a statement that meant little if workmen were behind the wall. The whole

episode remained controversial. The photography department
of a leading London weekly asserted emphatically that, after
submitting the photograph to minute scrutiny, there could be
only one conclusion: the brick could not have been thrown
through the window. Critics have suggested that Price's critical faculties had waned during his final years and that that
was why he included this obscure incident in his book; some
went even further and accused him of letting his desire for
publicity and his wish to increase the potential sales of his
book override the impartiality and personal integrity for
which he was so highly respected during much of his career.
Someone who knew him during this period has written:

> It was always my (doubtless incomplete) understanding that he
> was mainly interested in exposing various spurious manifestations
> but that somewhere along the line he found it more profitable
> or amusing to write about the lore itself rather than its possibly
> faked nature. I don't call him any more of a fraud than I would
> Professor Joad, with whom he was occasionally associated. I think
> both gentlemen were rather publicity-minded, that being largely
> their stock in trade.

By the time *The End of Borley Rectory* was published in
1946 the Rectory site had twice changed hands. The lower
part was occupied by Mr Tom Gooch, a local man, who built
himself a home on it. The northwest section of the grounds,
including the cottage and Rectory site, was first acquired by
a Mr Woods (who bought the ruins for demolition and sale of
bricks) and later by Captain Russell.

During this period Mr S. F. C. Kiernander (a knowledge-
able man on Borley) visited the ruins and talked to the
daughter of the owner, who was sceptical of the haunting.
Next day Mr Kiernander called for a final look before returning home. He was then told by the same girl that the previous
evening she had seen a figure by the old pump whose presence
'could not be explained in rational terms'. She thought that

the figure was 'certainly no human being' and so she had
considerably revised her opinion of the stories told about
mysterious figures at Borley.

While the property was owned, first by Mr Woods and
then by Captain Russell, the entire demolition of the Rectory
was completed and much of the material sold—some of it for
runways at nearby American Air Force bases. The war years
saw the end of Borley Rectory as a physical entity—though
the Borley story was far from finished.

# 5
# *Tunnels and Graves*

The excavations and probes at the Borley site have never been fully examined. There were six main episodes in this process: (1) the reputed finding of the 'tunnel' many years ago; (2) the digging up of the cats' cemetery; (3) the excavations of the cellars by Price; (4) digging and divining under the supervision of the late Reverend A. C. Henning; (5) digging during the Turners' occupancy; and (6) the extensive excavations since 1954, details of which have never been published before.

The first two were more probes or accidental explorations than systematic and properly-observed work. The first could be called a chance breaking into an apparent tunnel in the grounds of Borley Place by the late Mr Farrance, a local man (miscalled Tarrance in Price's books) while employed by the Reverend Harry Bull. While repairing a well, he came across some brickwork a few feet below ground. He forced an entrance and found that he had broken into what appeared to be a high and vaulted tunnel. He pursued it for some distance until he met 'foul air'; the candle he carried guttered and he was forced to turn back.

The still unexplained digging-up of the cats' cemetery was recorded by the late Sidney H. Glanville in his *Locked Book*. On his first visit to Borley on 18/19 June 1937 he noticed the graves of three cats in the garden, at the end of the Nun's

Walk, buried in the brambles. The headboards bore the names 'Gem', 'Rollo' and 'Sandy'. When he returned on 14/15 August 1937, Glanville saw that the grave marked 'Gem' had been considerably disturbed. It looked as if a large hole had been dug and the earth shovelled back, leaving a quantity of loose soil spread over a rough circle about five feet in diameter. Price told Glanville that he knew nothing about the digging. On a visit two weeks later when Glanville was accompanied by his son Roger, Captain H. G. Harrison and Squadron-Leader Horniman, the two Glanvilles dug up the grave again and turned up a considerable number of very large bones. Sidney Glanville told us that he felt they must have once belonged to the local butcher! (One of us— Peter Underwood—still remembers finding the skull of a cow lying near a hedge in the Rectory grounds during a visit in 1947.) Further digging was carried out in this area under the direction of Mr Henning in 1946 and 1947 following the curious reactions by a water-diviner, but nothing of interest was found.

The Price excavations in the Rectory cellar in 1943 were spread over three days. They began with the round well. After a mass of rubbish, including ashes, broken tiles and empty wine bottles had been removed, a sixteen-inch brass preserving pan was found. There followed more broken glass, a portion of a brass candlestick and miscellaneous rubbish. When a depth of five feet six inches was reached, a Sheffield plate milk or cream jug was discovered; when cleaned, it turned out to be in perfect condition. The floor of the entrance passage to the cellar was broken into and when the solid clayey marl below was excavated to a depth of three feet, parts of a skull were unearthed. Dr Eric Bailey, MRCS, LRCP, senior assistant pathologist of the County Hospital, Ashford, who was present, immediately identified the bones as human and thought they probably belonged to a woman. One or two ancient two-inch bricks were also found, together with pieces of broken clay pipes. Price suggested that these were probably made long before the Bull rectory was built on the site in 1863. Nothing more of interest was found that day.

During the next day's digging in the cellars the area was extended by several square yards and, penetrating to a depth of three feet, the usual broken tiles and other odds and ends were brought up. Then, sifting the detritus, a thin, oval-shaped piece of metal was found with a loop attached. Later tests proved it to be made of poor quality gold. A few minutes later, from the same part of the cellars, a small, thick, ovate plaque was dug up, also with an attached loop. After scrubbing, this plaque was found to be of copper, coated with a thick patina, much corroded and eaten away through long contact with the marl. Both objects were obviously pendants and bore religious symbols.

After careful cleaning and a visit to the Reverend Father M. J. Moriarty at Westminster Cathedral and consulting Messrs Maurice Vanpoulle, the church furnishers and Roman Catholic medallists, Price established that the plaque was a copy of the 'Miraculous Medal' first struck in France in 1832, following 'divine instructions' given to Zoë Labouré, afterwards the Blessed Catherine Labouré. The reverse bore the full figure of the Virgin Mary shown crushing the head of a serpent under her feet and surrounded by stars; the obverse was the monogram 'M' with two hearts, one pierced with a sword and surrounded by twelve stars; around the edge ran an invocation. The complete story of this medal formed Chapter IV of *The End of Borley Rectory*. The gold pendant was believed to be much older and probably of French origin. These pendants were buried with the skull fragments in Liston churchyard in May 1945.

Price returned to London on 19 August 1943. On 30 August Mr Sidney H. Glanville, his son, Squadron-Leader R. H.

Glanville, Mr and Mrs Henning and Price again visited the Rectory and had a day's digging but nothing of interest came to light. If the critics' hypothesis of Price having purposely planted the bones and duly found them were true, it is very difficult to explain this visit. Why should he continue his exertions when he had achieved his purpose? On the other hand, if the discoveries were genuine—as most people now seem to believe—it was natural that he should have another try in the hope of finding something more of interest. If he *had* planted the evidence, surely he would have seen to it that additional objects were discovered, thus strengthening his hand.

One of the long-standing mysteries of Borley involves conflicting statements about a crypt in Borley church. In 'The Most Haunted House in England' (p 50) Price stated that Miss Ethel Bull spoke of coffins in the crypt having been unaccountably moved on several occasions. Yet she told Peter Underwood that she knew nothing of a crypt at Borley and had not made the statement attributed to her. To add to the confusion, on 3 July 1972 Mr G. Croom-Hollingsworth told us that he held evidence about Miss Ethel Bull knowing all about the crypt and that she had been down the vault!

When Harry Price visited Borley on 27 August 1943 to investigate the cellars of the gutted Rectory, a careful search was made for any likely entrance to the church crypt. It was concluded that the opening might very well be under a heavy stone slab let into the central aisle, forming part of the flooring. It was obviously too large for an ancient memorial stone. The slab was raised from its bed (a layer of sand)—but unfortunately no further attempt was made to establish definitely whether or not there was any opening leading beneath the church. However, one important discovery was made: the stone had been laid upside down and was, in fact, the original pre-Reformation stone altar. After consulting Mr F. C. Eeles,

FSA, and the Reverend Montagu Benton, MA, FSA, Vicar of Fingringhoe and secretary of the Essex Archaeological Society, Mr Henning obtained a faculty from the chancellor of the diocese to have the altar restored. It was arranged that some boards in the Sanctuary should be removed as Mr Henning was anxious to know what was below them and they were to be replaced with stone flags in preparation for the mason to erect the pre-Reformation altar.

At last all was ready and excavation started on Whit Monday, 26 May 1947. Mr and Mrs Henning, aided by Mr James Turner and Mr J. Durrant, removed the altar cloth, the cross and candles and began to pull up the floor boards. Directly beneath them they found a black marble slab, evidently a tomb. Eventually they identified it as the tomb of the Reverend Humphrey Burrough, Rector of Borley from 1722 to 1757. It was in perfect condition. The headmastership of the Grammar School, Sudbury, was combined from 1714 until 1817 with the curacy of St Gregory's Church, Sudbury, where Burrough was listed as Rector in 1714. His most famous pupil was his nephew, Thomas Gainsborough, the painter, who was born at Sudbury.

The work continued. Mr Henning hoped to find the supporting pillars of the original altar but there was no trace of them and he concluded that they must have been broken up at the time the *mensa* was discarded. Whilst the sandy soil beneath the Sanctuary was being dug up, many bones, yellow and brittle with age, were found; they were collected in a basket and subsequently buried in Borley churchyard.

During the afternoon, while probing into the loose earth with a crowbar, Mr Turner broke into what proved to be a vault, presumably that of the Reverend Humphrey Borrough. The brickwork was in perfect condition—as if it had been built the day before. There was no escape of foul air; when a torch was lowered on the end of a pole, three skeletons were clearly seen, one on top of another, in some three feet of

water. They were presumed to be those of the Rector and his daughters; the wood of the coffins had been eaten away. Next day the hole was sealed and new flooring put down. At dusk the old wooden altar was taken in Mr Turner's car to Liston church.

On Monday 2 June, the masons completed their work and the altar (weighing fifteen hundredweight) was raised from the floor of the chancel and placed on four Portland stone pillars. At the same time the front choir stalls and communion rails were removed. The rededication of the altar took place on 15 June. It is perhaps well to remember that the beautiful little church at Borley is primarily a place of worship—and only incidentally an apparent centre of paranormal activity.

During 1946 and 1947 other digging and divining was carried out on the Rectory site under the direction of Mr Henning. The Rector thought that the lost plate of Borley church might well be buried in the grounds and his efforts were mainly directed to test this idea. Several holes were dug in places indicated by diviners, mostly on the lower, south-eastern part of the site, but nothing of interest was found.

Mr James Turner lived at the Rectory cottage from May 1947 to June 1950 and during this time carried out extensive explorations in the vicinity of the wells. Before he completely filled in the rubble-crammed cellars of the Rectory and laid out a sunken rose-garden, he and his friends spent considerable time in clearing the rubbish from the cellars and at length reached the round well where the cream jug had been discovered. As they uncovered the well, there was much escape of gas. Next day the well was broken into and dug out. There was nothing below but solid clay and though this, too, was excavated thoroughly, nothing interesting came to light. Before it was refilled, a photograph was taken of the excavated well.

The large, deep well was also investigated. It has a depth

of some eighty feet and water at seventy-one feet. The dangerous condition of its walls discouraged a number of explorers who were keen to extract any possible secret from this relic of the old Rectory. But Mr Turner has been down the well and tells us that there is definitely no tunnel leading off it as had been suggested. Many persistent reports of such a tunnel have cropped up over the years, suggesting that a tunnel led from a building which was presumed to have occupied the site of Borley Rectory to a nunnery or other building in the locality (some said, at Bures, but no valid evidence has ever been produced) or under the road to the church crypt. It had been suggested that a nunnery did exist at Bures and a local resident believed firmly that she possessed a photograph of it. This has not yet come to light and we have been unable to trace any proof of such a convent. J. A. E. Kitchen, in an article on Bures published in the *East Anglian Magazine* in August 1955, referred to an old corner grocery store, now a cafe, that used to be a fascinating old place, full of huge oak beams and with unexpected steps to different levels. Legend had it that a tunnel led from under the shop to the reputedly haunted Borley Rectory—but a legend it remained, without substantiation.

A depression in the side of the large well was visible from ground level, but when Mr Turner reached that part of its wall, he found nothing more and the brickwork was intact. The existence of tunnels in the vicinity, however, can hardly be disputed. We have mentioned Mr Farrance's experience at Borley Place; and while at Borley in 1950, Peter Underwood made a number of tests that convinced those present of the existence of hollows of some sort under the road outside the main entrance to the Borley site. The late Mr J. Granville Squiers, author of *Secret Hiding Places* (London, 1932) explained at a Ghost Club meeting that such hollows are often well-constructed sewers and sometimes were used as tunnels and hiding places in later years.

In October 1954 Mr Philip Paul spent a week at Borley, looking for the tunnels. He discussed his plans and difficulties with Peter Underwood and he was given a copy of a rough sketch map showing the reputed location of the Borley tunnels. Digging duly took place; it began in the farmyard near Borley Place. It was here, in the garden, that Mr Farrance had broken into an apparent tunnel some thirty years earlier. After hard work a dome was uncovered but it proved to be only the cover of a well.

Mr Paul had four main objectives. He wanted to find the rest of the 'Nun's' skeleton; he hoped to break into one of the tunnels which undoubtedly existed thereabouts; he was looking for confirmatory evidence that the Rectory garden had once formed part of a plague pit; and finally he kept in mind the lost plate of Borley church. He arranged for the digging of three holes on the Rectory site. A number of large bones were dug up and a mass of rubble and rubbish shifted but no tunnels were encountered. One hole, about a foot square, penetrated to a depth of four feet below the old cellar floor and here the diggers seemed to be on ground that had never been disturbed before.

During these 1954 excavations a curious story was circulated to the effect that at the time of the demolition of the Rectory some locked iron gates had been discovered behind a wall in the cellars. It was rumoured that these gates were taken off their hinges but there was 'nothing' behind them. There appears to be little if any foundation for this story. Certainly, Miss Ethel Bull said she had no recollection of any iron gates in the Borley Rectory cellars.

The Philip Paul excavations were continued in July 1955. The weather was perfect and the work included the thorough exploration of the entrance passage wall on the road side. This was a logical consequence of the story of the iron gates which arose during the earlier digging. On 14 July 1955, the Reverend J. C. Dening, who took part in that year's excavations, told Peter Underwood that the existence of such iron gates was most unlikely in that part of the cellar where they would have had to be if they had formed the entrance to a tunnel running in the direction of Borley church. During the 1955 diggings a few bones, clearly animal in origin, were discovered. Perhaps the most interesting event was the unearthing of a fairly large block of the old pre-1772-type two-inch bricks, establishing almost beyond doubt the existence of a much earlier house in the immediate locality. During 1955 much of the entrance passage of the cellar where Price found the human remains was cleared to floor level.

Early in 1956, diggings was resumed by Mr L. Sewell (living then at Long Melford), who had been interested in Borley for many years and who had taken a leading part in the recent work. Before the wet summer a depth of two feet below floor level was reached.

During August 1956 Mr Philip Paul appealed for help and was offered the use of a mechanical digger. With the aid of this machine a good deal of the rubbish was excavated and the floor ripped up in one or two places. Following this activity and some publicity of dubious value, Mr Paul became convinced that nothing more of interest would be discovered and that there was no point in spending more time and effort on the site.

A number of local volunteers who had assisted at the digging now declared their wish to continue and the owners of the site very kindly agreed to this. The greater part of the work was done by Mr Sewell and Mr L. G. Rayner of Ipswich; others who visited the site and assisted in various ways included the Reverend John C. Dening, Mr S. F. C. Kiernander, Mr G. Lambert of Bury St Edmunds and Messrs C. Botwright, O. Parker, G. Ward and F. Whittle of Ipswich. The work continued at week-ends until the approach of winter. The site still attracted a great number of visitors from all parts of the country, and interest appeared to be as strong as ever. During this period almost the entire cellar floor was cleared and remains of the brick wine bins were exposed. Much of the cellar area was filled with old iron and other rubbish but the contents of the part which had been under the front of the house consisted mainly of debris from the vanished Rectory. Many interesting relics came to light—among them a lot of white marble fragments, presumably portions of a fireplace or fireplaces; fittings belonging to the famous bells, charred beams and two curiosities in the shape of a horseshoe, dated by an expert as *circa* 1600 (this came from below the floor of the Rectory cellars) and an egg-cup bearing the arms of Pembroke College, Cambridge. The latter had probably belonged to the late Reverend L. A. Foyster, a Pembroke man.

It was only after it had been decided to finish work for the season and tidying up began that another interesting discovery was made. At the end of the passage, near the entrance to the wine cellar, some brickwork was found that proved to be another well. Filled in, of course, it was partly underneath the wine cellar wall and must have belonged to a previous house. Work was resumed and the well cleared to a depth of four feet when water began to seep in, and in view of the approaching winter months it was decided to postpone further exploration until 1957. The contents of the well included two-inch bricks, tiles, oyster shells and pieces of plaster. Before the workers retired for the season they carefully covered and sealed the well.

In a letter dated 20 May 1957, Mr Sewell pointed out that in his opinion Price's excavation did not seem to bear out Price's contention that the odd shape of the cellars was due to their being part of a previous building that once occupied the site—probably a rectory belonging to the Herringham family whose memorials can be seen in Borley church. The 'angle wall' where the wine bins were, Mr Sewell said, did not rest on ancient foundations—in fact, it had no foundations at

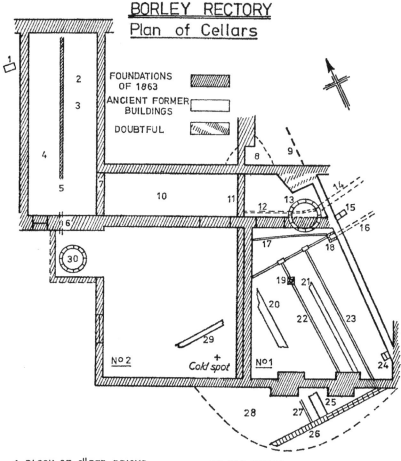

# BORLEY RECTORY
## Plan of Cellars

FOUNDATIONS
OF 1863

ANCIENT FORMER
BUILDINGS

DOUBTFUL

1
2
3
4
5
7
8
9
6
10
11
12
13
14
15
16
17
18
19
20
21
22
23
24
25
26
27
28
29
30

No 2
No 1
+
Cold spot

1 BLOCK OF 2" RED BRICKS
2 EXCAVATED 1956
3 ENTRANCE, SITE OF STAIRS
4 MODERN DRAIN PIPES 3" DIA
5 PIPES MISSING HERE
6 DRAIN CONTINUES THROUGH WALL
7 WALL UNDER FLOOR
8 RUBBLE FILLING, BRICKS & TILES
9 LINE OF HARD CLAY
10 EXCAVATED 1958
11 WALL UNDER FLOOR
12 DRAIN, LARGE OLD PIPES
13 FILLED-IN WELL
14 OLD DRAIN
15 FRAGMENTARY WALL

16 OLD DRAIN
17 DRAIN D PIPES OLD TYPE
18 MODERN COVERED DRAIN
19 APPARENTLY LATER INSERTION
20 WALL OF 2" RED BRICKS
21 RED UN-GLAZED TILES
22/23 OLD DRAIN PIPES, FLAT
BOTTOMS 12" BELOW FLOOR
24 BLOCK OF 2" RED BRICKS
25 WALL OF 2" RED BRICKS
26 FLAT YELLOW BRICKS
27 DRAIN
28 RUBBLE FILLING BRICKS & TILES
29 FOUNDATION DISCOVERED 1937
30 SITE OF WELL

Plan of the cellars on the site of Borley Rectory

all and the two-inch bricks there were lined with concrete similar to the other walls. Later discoveries, however, caused Mr Sewell to change his views and he came to agree with Price. The odd shape of the wall appeared to follow the line of an earlier building but was not an original wall. Mr Sewell added that although half the cellar entrance passage was excavated to a depth of five feet, no human remains were found. However, various fossils were dug up together with part of an Iron Age quern, a hand-mill for grinding corn and other grains. The excavation was restarted and continued below floor level.

During this period quite a lot of Rectory 'relics' were discovered, including one of the bells which was cleaned and mounted as an ornament for the Rectory cottage. Some people hope that one day it may ring again without human agency . . .

On 21 September 1957, Mr Sewell told of a further discovery. Having found the base of the cellar wall on the south side, the excavators cut back the bank and discovered that the eastern end was mostly composed of dry rubble with numerous two-inch bricks, tiles and other oddments. Outside the cellar wall, at the other end, they found another wall, or rather a row of bricks, running out at right angles to the 'wine bin' wall. These two rows of bricks lay flat on the ground, side by side, and did not appear to have had any mortar on them at all. They were without frogs, about two-and-a-half inches thick. They ran on into the bank where it was difficult to dig further as the earth had been piled up there some twelve to fifteen feet above the level of the cellar floor. Later, however, it was possible to undercut this bank. It was then found that at a point seven feet six inches from the start of the wall another course of bricks, placed crosswise and properly cemented, had been laid on these bricks, making a finished wall. Where the bricks disappeared into the bank still another wall was found running at right angles and therefore parallel

with the 'wine bin' wall. This was composed of soft red bricks
properly laid and mortared, about fourteen inches wide and
two feet long, roughly cut off where it almost touched the
cellar wall. It would appear that this thick red brick wall was
one of the main supporting walls of a previous house while
the thinner walls belonged to cellars. The distance between
the red brick and the parallel 'wine bine' wall was roughly ten
feet, wide enough to form a cellar. It looked as if this red brick
wall was roughly cut through to make way for the cellar wall
of the Bull rectory on the inside of which the mechanical
digger had operated. But there may be further traces in the
centre part of the cellar below floor level. These walls clearly
had nothing to do with the Bull rectory except that they 'tied
up' with the 'wine bin' wall which appeared, for the most part
at any rate, to be a rebuilt one. Neither did they have anything to do with the Herringham rectory, for this stood farther west. This would seem to bear out Mr Sewell's theory
that a still earlier building was demolished when the Herringham rectory was built.

On 2 July 1957, the Reverend John C. Dening, on his way
back to Bournemouth after a weekend at Borley, met Peter
Underwood in London. He revealed that Mr Sewell had succeeded in discovering a map showing a house that had once
occupied the site of Borley Rectory. For over twenty-five years
all students of the Borley haunting had searched for some
definite record of such a building. Physical traces of a former
house (or perhaps houses) had been found but we were totally
without any documentary evidence until Mr Sewell's triumph
in locating a Tithe Map for 1841. This shows the Rectory cottage or coach-house occupying its present position; but it
must have been re-built or at least re-faced to bring it into
harmony with the architectural style of the Bull rectory. The
Herringham rectory of the map is shown standing further
west and occupying a much smaller area than the huge building erected by the Reverend H. D. E. Bull. A pond is marked

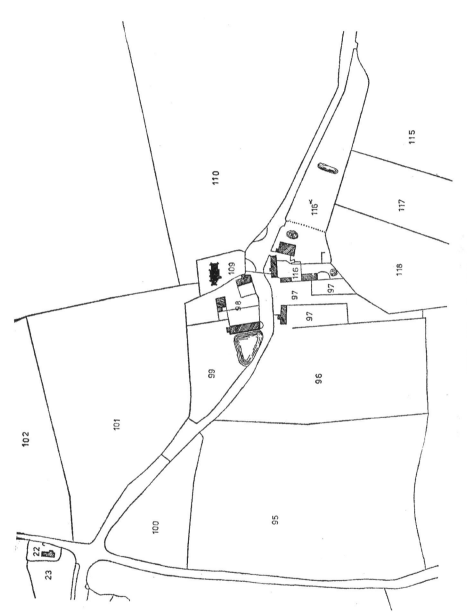

Tithe Map for 1841

in front of the Rectory, to the east of it. This pond was on the site of the present cellars and Mr Sewell suggested that when the earlier building was demolished, its cellars—which may or may not have been filled in—eventually became a pond. Later, when the Bull rectory was built, they were utilised again as part of the 'large and rambling cellars' described by Price. The Herringham rectory did not appear to be ancient, for White's *Gazetteer* for 1848 identifies the incumbent as the Reverend J. P. Herringham 'who has a good modern residence'. Perhaps the Reverend W. Herringham built this rectory when he came to the parish in 1807. Mr Sewell also discovered a map dated 1772 which showed three buildings on the site, each separately enclosed. The centre building appeared to abut on the road and could very well be the forerunner of the present Rectory cottage. If this were so, then the building to the south-east would be on the site of the present cellars and the other building, to the west, would be practically in line with the tunnel that was finally discovered.

During the wekend of 29 June-2 July 1957, more remains of the foundations of a previous building were found. The bricks were not the ancient two-inch variety and the structure, evidently part of a wall, had no connection with the foundations of the Bull rectory; in fact, this fragmentary wall had been built at such an odd angle and was of such a peculiar shape that the diggers were at a loss to account for its purpose. It appeared to be heading for the corner where the latest well was discovered, but there was a definite gap. It was at the end of the passage near the 'angle buttress' and the only place where all the cellar wall was missing. The mysterious story of the iron gates again came to the diggers' minds, but nothing was found that might have established their existence or settled the problem one way or the other.

On 12 September 1957 came the discovery of the long-lost and eagerly-sought tunnel running under the road between the vanished Rectory and Borley church or Borley Place.

Workmen employed by Messrs Biggs Wall, contractors to Halstead Rural District Council, digging a trench from the direction of Borley Green towards Rodbridge Corner in order to lay water mains in the parish, cut through brickwork at about 9am with their mechanical digger and came upon the tunnel. Mr Sewell was promptly informed and immediately went to Borley with Mr W. J. Leathley of the *East Anglian Daily Times* and Mr Leathley's son.

The contractors digging the trench had kept the place open and Mr Sewell and his friends were able to make an immediate and thorough examination. (We are indebted to Mr Sewell for his clear and lucid reports of the excavation of the tunnel.)

Until this point the general inference placed the tunnel, if one existed, running in an east-west direction. In fact, it was found to be running roughly north-south, some two or three yards west of the barn in front of Borley Place; the trench dug by the water main contractors was on the south side of the road.

The position of the tunnel could account for many reports of a hollow sound noticed by drivers of farm carts and other vehicles on this stretch of road and for the results of experiments conducted in March 1950 when Peter Underwood became convinced that tunnels or drains of some kind existed here. Unfortunately it had been impossible at the time to obtain permission for digging near the churchyard parallel with the road.

Mr Sewell entered the tunnel and examined it carefully, but his first impression was that it held nothing of great interest—certainly no trace of any church plate. There was a flat brick floor covered with hard earth, upright walls about a foot high and a domed or arched roof. The bricks were of the red two-inch Tudor type, the whole construction strongly built and the roof still very clean. Mr Sewell made careful measurements and found that the width of the tunnel was thirty-two inches and its height twenty-eight inches. The top was twelve inches below the road surface, including three inches of metalling. As Mr Sewell pointed out, it had stood up remarkably well to the regular passage of heavy agricultural machinery. The tunnel was found to continue for several yards beyond the road on both sides. The northern end was blocked by a brick wall and the southern by an accumulation of earth that reached almost to the roof. At the Borley Place end a drainpipe had been inserted into the modern wall and this was the probable cause of earth and rubbish being washed down. Mr Sewell's party took some excellent photographs and returned to Sudbury. That evening Mr Sewell saw Mr and Mrs Payne of Borley Place who were very interested in the discovery and kindly gave their permission for investigation on their property on either side of the road.

The following Saturday Mr Sewell continued his exploration and uncovered the roof of the tunnel only a few inches below the surface amongst the young fir trees on the south side of the road, tracing it for some twenty feet. At this point a deep ditch ran at right angles to the tunnel, several feet deeper. The end of the tunnel did not have a finished appearance but followed roughly the slope of the bank. This suggested that the tunnel was cut through when the ditch was dug although the end of the tunnel might have collapsed at some time. It was not established when the ditch was dug; it does not seem to be marked on the Tithe Map of 1841. The end of the tunnel was uncovered by digging; it was found to be packed so hard with earth that it was impossible to get even a fork into it. Later many pieces of broken bottles, crockery and odds and ends of recent date were unearthed. Mr Sewell concentrated on working at this section most of the Saturday and reached the brick floor but did not penetrate very far.

Next day Mr Sewell and Mr L. G. Rayner continued their exploration. They found the roof of the tunnel only a few inches below the surface inside the farmyard. Mr Rayner quickly removed some bricks and inspected the interior. They found themselves very close to the blocking brick wall; these bricks, made by Byford of Melford, were quite modern. When they removed two or three of these bricks, they discovered that here the tunnel had collapsed and was filled with earth and stones. At this point there was some six inches of earth on its floor. Removing this obstruction they were at last able to traverse the length of the tunnel for the whole width of the road and up to the point where the contractors had filled in their trench. Near the farmyard wall, on the roadside, where the modern drainpipe had been inserted, they made another interesting discovery. Under the grass verge between the road and the wall, the tunnel dipped several inches in the direction of Borley Place. This did not seem to be due to subsidence. The tunnel began perfectly level under the road; it then suddenly sloped down for a yard or so and then continued level again. This difference in direction applied to roof, walls and floor; the photographs showed it clearly. There was no sign of any large cracks as there would have been with subsidence. Curiously enough, the dip appeared to follow the contour of the land, for the farmyard lies lower than the road. This rules out the possibility of the tunnel having been originally a large drain, as a local surveyor suggested.

Mr Sewell and Mr Rayner explored near the farther farmyard wall and found the tunnel here, too, in a collapsed state; apparently it had subsided or had been filled in throughout the length of the farmyard. They also dug on the other side of the wall, within the garden of Borley Place, and again found traces of the tunnel, turning up several two-inch bricks. From here to the end of the tunnel the distance was roughly ninety feet. If the tunnel had continued straight on it would have entered the ancient cellars of Borley Place where there was a curious square alcove, its base about three feet below the outside floor level. On its way the tunnel would have hit (or possibly just missed) the well in the garden where, according to reports, it was penetrated many years earlier by the late Mr Farrance.

Following their thorough exploration, Mr Sewell and Mr Rayner covered the opening they had made and filled in the hole. Their work by no means answered all the questions the Borley hauntings had raised but opened up new possibilities, new explanations and theories.

It is doubtful, however, whether a great deal more digging will be done at Borley. The entire cellar floor and the cellar passage have been excavated to a depth of about four feet with nothing of interest to show for a vast amount of hard work—except some belemnites and other fossils at a depth of three feet where the soil appeared to be undisturbed. The main walls continued underneath the floor—or rather, the passage walls seemed to go through the main walls. Digging in the old wine cellars where the floor bricks had been removed the previous year, some three or four inches of sandy gravel were discovered and then, in the clay, a series of drains of the ancient type, with a flat bottom. A row of flat tiles, red and fairly thin, were simply laid, quite level, on the clay, apparently free of mortar. Curiously enough, similar tiles were found beneath the 'wine bin' wall, the bottom of which was then exposed; this wall had no foundation or footings. These tiles were subsequently cleaned and found to be oblong roofing tiles. More of the red brick wall uncovered the previous year outside the wine cellar also came to light, and since the wall and the drains all seemed to be in their original position and to be completely undisturbed Mr Sewell decided that he and his helpers were unlikely to find anything of interest beneath them. Some of the drains were set in a small trench filled with flint, so the drainage should have been excellent. There still remains, however, the possibility of discovering just where and how far the tunnel continues or continued on the Rectory side. Future digging might reveal other secrets of the past in the locality; and, as so often in the long history of investigations at Borley, instead of the end of the story all this extensive work might very well prove to be merely the end of a chapter.

# 6
# *The Haunting of Borley Church*

Borley's attractive twelfth-century church stands just across the road from the main entrance to the site of vanished Borley Rectory. As in the case of some twenty-five other churches in Essex, its dedication is unknown though the late Reverend A. C. Henning told us he thought it may have been to St. Andrew. The vicinity of Borley church, where so many of the chief actors of the Borley story lie buried, has itself been the scene of a number of strange happenings during recent years.

In this, of course, it is by no means unique—curious and possibly paranormal incidents have been reported from many churches in the British Isles and elsewhere. To give only a few examples showing similarity to the Borley reports: an eleventh-century church near Bristol has long attracted psychical researchers; a 'little brown lady' has been seen there, and mysterious footsteps and unexplained whispers have been heard on many occasions. Ghostly footsteps have been the feature at the church of St Bartholomew the Great, Smithfield, which are supposed to be those of the founder of the church, Rahere, one of Henry I's courtiers. When Dr Oskar Goldberg visited England as a member of the United Nations Association, he told the inside story of the haunting associated with the church of St Nicholas, Millvale, Pittsburgh, Pennsylvania. Knocks and clicks were heard and 'an apparition' seen on many occasions some years ago. Holy Trinity Church, Micklegate, York, had a hooded ghost believed to be the last abbess of the convent formerly attached to the building. Miss Christina Hole has told us about the unaccountable organ music reported from Avenbury church, Herefordshire. Similar music has been heard in a number of other churches. A hooded figure was also seen at St Mary's collegiate church, Port Elizabeth, South Africa, where 'muted' organ music was reported to be heard continually at one time.

Before examining the varied and frequently well-documented reports of happenings which have been described as 'outside normality' and witnessed in the vicinity of Borley church, let us look at the building itself.

In *A Short History of Borley and Liston Churches* (1937) Mr J. M. Bull described the church as small and consisting of a chancel and nave with south porch and west tower. It is composed chiefly of flint rubble. Mr Bull thought it probable that a church was built on the site in the twelfth century, consisting of chancel and nave of the same length as the present ones. After the chancel and north wall deteriorated, they were rebuilt about 1500 when the tower and brick south porch were added. The small original windows were replaced by the present ones during the fourteenth and fifteenth centuries. The middle window in the north wall of the nave is now the earliest, dating from the fourteenth century, preserved probably when the wall was rebuilt. The three-stage tower has gargoyles projecting from each of the four sides. The doorway to the staircase is just past the tower arch. The winding steps are worn by many feet and the top provides an excellent panoramic view of the surrounding countryside.

Inside the church there are two monuments dedicated to the Waldegraves, for generations a family of considerable importance in the neighbourhood and both good examples of sixteenth-century sculpture. The foremost is the large and impressive Waldegrave monument at the east end of the nave. Sir Edward Waldegrave died in 1561; his wife Frances survived him by thirty-eight years. Their effigies lie side by side; Sir Edward in armour, his head resting on his helmet; his wife in a tight-fitting bodice and skirt, a flat cap on her head, wearing a large ruff, with a squirrel (the emblem of thrift) at her feet. These effigies were usually made in the lifetime of their originals and were supposed to be faithul reproductions of them in the prime of life. An ornate stone canopy supported by six marble pillars covers the figures and the three sons and three daughters of the marriage can be seen on the sides. The family arms are represented in relief on the canopy and on the edge, which is of black marble, there is a Latin inscription; a rough English translation runs:

> Edward died in the year of our Lord one thousand five hundred and sixty-one, in the forty-fourth year of his age on the first day of September. Frances died in the year of our Lord one thousand five hundred and ninety-nine, seventy years of age, on the eighteenth day of October. Lo! within this tomb lies Edward Waldegrave and with him Frances, formerly the companion of his bed, but now of his grave. A family untouched by misfortune. Behold, O man, what honours, what descent, what wealth will profit thee, when breath of life shall leave thy frame! Thou seest nothing remain when the structure of man is dissolved. Earth its part reclaims, and so doth heaven.

The other Waldegrave monument was put up to the memory of Sir Edward's third daughter, Magdala, in 1598. It consists of a tablet bearing her effigy, set into the north wall of the chancel. She is shown kneeling on a cushion with an open book before her, wearing a tight-fitting bodice, a loose skirt, a sleeveless mantle over her shoulders and a ruff. Above her head are cherubs encircled with rays of glory. The indent of a brass can be seen near the east end of the nave; it probably dates from the fifteenth century.

The Borley registers date from 1652 for baptisms, 1656 for burials and 1709 for marriages. Up to 1710 they are preserved in a transcript made from an older book now missing. They contain no mention of any Waldegrave.

A number of attractive yew trees stand in the churchyard, bordering the path leading to the church. On a visit to Chilton Lodge, the late Miss Ethel Bull showed Peter Underwood an old watercolour sketch of Borley church with the path from the road shown in a different place from the existing one—though this may have been the artist's transposition. The graves in the churchyard include those of the Reverend Henry Dawson Ellis Bull (who built Borley Rectory in 1863), his son, the Reverend Henry (Harry) Foyster Bull who succeeded his father in 1892, and Mrs Bull, wife of H. D. E. Bull.

The church is close to Borley Place, formerly Borley Manor House, now the residence of the Payne family. The two first-storey windows overlooking the churchyard are dummies.

One of the earliest incidents reported in the church was told by the Reverend Harry Bull to Mr E. R. Ambrose of Sudbury, who was organist at Borley church for sixteen years before the first world war. Mr Ambrose often visited the place after he ceased to be regularly attached to it. It was in the middle of the summer of 1920 that he heard the story from the Reverend Harry Bull. While the latter was in the church with a gentleman friend, they both heard a loud tapping noise which started outside. Then the sounds seemed to enter the building; the Rector and his friend followed them all round the inside wall. They went outside but could find nothing to explain the origin of the sounds.

Harry Price recounted a few incidents connected with Borley church and its immediate neighbourhood in his two books devoted to the haunting. On Saturday 20 November 1937 Mr S. H. Glanville and Dr H. F. Bellamy visited Borley for an observational period at the Rectory. This was during the

year Price rented the place. When the Glanville party arrived
on the Saturday morning, they found painters at work on the
outside of the Rectory. The foreman was a Mr Hardy who
was born and had spent his life at Borley. He told Mr Glanville about his son, aged nineteen, who when returning home
from work about a fortnight before, had heard singing or
chanting coming from the church as he passed it. The church
was locked at the time and he did not stop to investigate.

Such chanting inside a locked and empty church has been
reported on a number of occasions and in several places. The
Reverend H. S. Cheales, of The Rectory, Wyck Rissington,
described his experiences in a letter:

> ... on separate occasions my wife and I have both heard singing
> from inside our beautiful old church here (similar to the Borley
> Church experiences) when we have been in the churchyard. It
> seems to be of a medieval character; plainsong chanting. I sup-
> pose it is a relic of worship hundreds of years old which still
> lingers on . . .

Similar chanting (by a single female voice) has been reported from Langenhoe church, Essex, by a former rector
and other witnesses; a haunting that may be linked to the
Borley case for there are associations with the Waldegraves
and combined livings of the parishes for two periods.

The late Reverend A. C. Henning wrote to Harry Price on
16 April 1942 speaking about the displacement of certain
objects in Borley church, including that of the sanctuary
lamp kept burning near the tabernacle on the altar. A Mrs
Pearson looked after it, lighting the small wick every morning and putting it out at night. For about a fortnight the wick
was frequently found to have been moved. Mrs Pearson mentioned the matter to Mr Henning who suggested putting a
book or some other cover over the lamp glass. That evening
she placed a psalter over the glass, the light was put out and
the church was locked for the night. Next morning the book

was found on the floor—although both church doors were locked and no one could have got in during the night. Afterwards the cover of a book that had become detached was put over the lamp but this, too, was shifted on two occasions. Mr Henning added that while there might have been some natural explanation, he did not see how anything like a bird or bat could remove the book and cover—or had any cause for doing so. Mrs Pearson, in fact, kept a look out for a bird but never saw one inside the church.

On 21 April 1946 Mr John Durrant of Ballingdon Street, Sudbury, visited Borley, primarily to inspect the church. He was a keen archaeologist and naturalist. He gave the following account of his experiences:

> My fiancée and I had looked all over the church and we were standing near the south door—I was actually signing the Visitors' Book—when we both heard footsteps in the porch and also the 'snack' [Suffolk term for 'latch'] moving. I remarked: 'Some more visitors.' The door did not open and thinking that these people were trying to enter and the door sticking, I went to open it from the inside. To my amazement there was no person there and I quickly ran round the church and down the road but there was no person in sight. There the matter rested until I read *The End of Borley Rectory* and learned that strange things had happened in the church. My fiancée is a Sister at a Newmarket hospital and not an 'imaginative' type.

Other people also heard footsteps in the vicinity of the church. In one of his letters to Harry Price, Mr Henning gave details of a strange incident connected with a catechism class in 1946. On that particular Sunday the children arrived early and sat down to wait for their teacher, a Miss Byford. Presently they heard footsteps come up the path to the church and the sound of the key turning in the door. Kathleen Finch, a girl of about thirteen, immediately went to the door and called out to Miss Byford. There was no reply. After a few minutes the teacher arrived and was astonished to find the door locked. There was no satisfactory explanation found for this event. Mr Henning also spoke of Mr Durrant paying another visit to Borley on a Sunday. While he walked away, about half-way down the path, he heard a loud and distinct 'bang' from the direction of the priest's door leading into the sanctuary. There was no one inside the place at the time.

Writing from Antrim Road, Shoeburyness, Donald W. L. Newland, BA, lecturer in history and current affairs at the Municipal College, Southend-on-Sea, recounted in his letter, dated 11 April 1947, hearing an entirely different noise. It was 'like earth falling' and quite distinct, coming from the Waldegrave monument. There was no apparent external cause such as mice, birds or workmen. 'I thought the sounds might be subjective,' Mr Newland wrote, 'but they repeated themselves on my returning to the church after leaving it to investigate the exterior. I also recollect it was very chilly in the church although the outside temperature must have been between 55° and 60° F.'

Mrs Harry Bull, on a visit to the Borley district, had arranged with Mr Henning to decorate the church with flowers on Easter Sunday 1947—as a somewhat nostalgic gesture to invoke her family's long association with the place. On the Saturday she spent a long time at the church, and the Rector who called in as he was passing congratulated her on the beauty of her arrangements. Next morning the flowers were found scattered all over the interior though the church had been locked during the night.

In May 1947 Mr James Turner, the poet and writer, purchased the cottage and the greater part of the old Rectory grounds, including the whole of the site of the Rectory itself. Peter Underwood visited Borley on 17 and 18 May, spending the night in the vicinity of the cottage and church. A planchette prediction in March 1938 had been fulfilled by the destruction of the Rectory by fire in 1939. Eight years later, there was talk of a new prediction by the same means, foretelling that Borley church would also be burned down 'during the month of September'. But the charming little church still stands unharmed a quarter of a century later.

On Wednesday 4 June 1947, Harry Price visited Borley church to see the recently restored pre-Reformation altar before giving a lecture at Sudbury on the Borley hauntings. He arrived at 5.30pm. Accompanied by Mr and Mrs Henning, Price walked up the chancel, leaving the west door open. They had been examining the tomb in the sanctuary and had just stepped back when they were surprised to hear loud and unbroken screeching of birds from the west end of the church. As the screeching died down, footsteps were heard approaching and entering the church. Thinking that visitors had come to see the altar, Mr Henning went to the door—but no one was visible. All three of those present had plainly heard the footsteps. A search of the grounds and roadway revealed no clue.

Some three weeks later, on 29 June 1947, Mr Anthony G. Smith of Bishop's Stortford College, described in a letter a visit he paid to Borley earlier in the year:

> On my first visit to Borley at Eastertime I was signing the Visitors' Book when I heard footsteps, ladies' footsteps, approaching the porch. They came as far as the door, or seemed to, and then stopped. I went to the door at once, but there was no one to be seen anywhere.

One day during the autumn of the same year, Miss Backhouse, headmistress of a nearby school, visited Borley to look at the restored altar. As she entered the church she became conscious of a 'presence' near her and as she walked up to the chancel step, limping footsteps followed her. Miss Backhouse, who wore rubber-soled shoes and was walking on the matting, turned and went out of the church. Again the footsteps followed her but only as far as the door. Outside in the churchyard all was quiet.

In a letter of 1 November 1947, James Turner mentioned a rather alarming experience he had in Borley churchyard on 2 August 1947. Strolling over to the church soon after midnight, he sat on the step of the priest's door for about three-quarters of an hour; at all events he heard Sudbury clock strike one before he suddenly became aware of 'something' coming up the main path. He saw nothing but plainly heard 'something or somebody with a lame leg and a swishing skirt' pass along the path towards the porch. He was relieved to hear the footsteps move towards the porch and not turn down the path towards him—a very understandable emotion. Later he added that the experience did not alarm him until afterwards, 'for it was a night of the full moon and there was not a breath of wind'. (Many of the alleged paranormal occurrences at Borley took place when the moon was full or on the wane, a time long considered by the superstitious as the most favourable time for casting spells and making incantations.)

About six weeks later, on 15 September 1947, Mr John May of Bury St Edmunds visited Borley as he wanted to see the scene of the hauntings by night. Until then he had only seen the church and churchyard under a hot summer sun and he thought that a 'ghost might be extremely difficult to see in the hard light of day!' His report continued:

> At 10.30 p.m. I leaned my bicycle against the stone wall of the churchyard, and stood for a few moments, looking up the path towards the porch and door. I could just see the dusty white of the gravel path, the dim blurred outlines of the yew trees that bordered it, and the shape of the gabled porch. The people retire to bed early in the country, and I saw not a soul; I went in crêpe-soled shoes to the porch and sat down upon a seat and began my vigil. Presently a crescent moon gave just enough light for me to see objects fairly clearly. Several times I looked at my watch. A few nesting birds rustled in the trees and the creeper that clothed the wall of the house adjoining the churchyard. There was the occasional lowing of cattle in the meadows near the river, and the hoot of an owl somewhere in the distance. That

was all—in between the sounds there was complete silence.

It was a warm summer night—there was no breath of wind. I looked at my watch, it was 11.43 p.m. Then I think I must have dozed. I jerked awake—because I had heard the latch on the churchyard gate click. The time was 12.16 a.m.

I do not think I was actually afraid, but I *was* aware of a certain amount of fear: the doubting sensation with which one probes the unknown, the caution with which one accepts a bargain from a stranger. Then I heard steps coming up the path. They paused for a second near one of the yew bushes. The light was clear. The footsteps continued but there was no one near. I sensed someone passing me, there was a chilliness in the air and I felt a slight pressure. Whatever it was I knew and felt that it was essentially EVIL. I also knew that I resented in some way hearing and not seeing. I then heard the sound of a key in the lock, then the creak of the door hinges as the door opened. I heard the door close. A few seconds later I heard soft notes and chords from the organ. The time was 12.18.

The music was not in any sequence of notes so as to form a conventional tune, just a jumble of atonal chords (I detest the 'modern' music of Hindemith and Honegger and I remember thinking that this music was similar to theirs). I sat on until 2.30 a.m. but heard nothing more—not even the opening of the door again. I went to look at the organ a few days afterwards. It was rather small for a church organ and I recall thinking it was rather a mean instrument for such an important visitor as a ghost . . .

Similar 'music' has been reported from a number of churches. It was heard with the sound of chanting at a church near Guildford in Surrey, and in 1950 voluntaries were repeatedly heard from the locked and empty parish church of Cressing, near Braintree, Essex, less than twenty miles from Borley.

In July 1948 Peter Underwood called at Liston Rectory and during his visit Mr Henning related several incidents involving the church, himself and his son, Stephen. On one occasion the two Hennings went to the church to arrange the flowers. They left a bottle of water on the seat in the porch.

While they were inside, they heard a 'bang' as if the bottle had fallen without breaking. Stephen wanted to rush to the porch and investigate but his father thought it best to wait for a few minutes as it occurred to him that they might hear footsteps. Presently Stephen walked to the west end of the church and, *without going out of the door,* saw the bottle still standing where it had been placed. He returned to join his father; after about two minutes both of them went into the porch and found that the bottle had been moved from the centre of the seat to the end near the open door. Apart from the 'bang' no noise of any kind was heard and the church door was open all the time.

About a week later Mr Henning and his son again went to the church for the same purpose. This time Stephen left his cap on the seat close to the porch entrance and special notice was taken of its exact position. After doing the flowers in the vestry, Mr Henning glanced into the porch and saw that the cap had moved to the centre of the seat. He insisted on being quite certain that there was insufficient wind to move the cap. Subsequently, the Rector several times placed his hat or Stephen's cap on the same seat—but nothing unusual happened.

About midway through October 1947, Mr Henning told us, Mrs Norah Walrond (Norah Burke, the novelist) of Thorne Lodge, Cookfield, Suffolk, had visited Borley to see the restored altar. She and the Rector were about half-way along the path when Mrs Walrond said 'The organ is playing!' They went inside but there was no one there and the organ was locked. They walked up and down the church path several times but there were no sounds except the hum of two tractors at work and a distant aeroplane—nothing remotely like the playing of an organ which they had both heard distinctly. A letter dated 27 October 1947 from Mrs Walrond gave an independent account of this experience. Mrs Walrond wrote:

I have known Borley Rectory and almost all the people in it and my knowledge of it extends over twenty years, but I have never before seen or heard any paranormal occurrence there, though I have been there innumerable times. Mr Henning said he would show me the newly created Mensa, so one day last week (the 15th I think it was) I went over and we got to the church about 3.15 p.m. As we were walking up the path to the south door (the path on which the footsteps were heard) I stopped and said, 'The organ is playing'. My first thought was that there was a service in progress and that therefore we could not go in. Mr Henning stopped and looked at me. He heard it too. He of course knew that there was no service going on. He darted forward and hurried into the church. I followed but hung back because I still thought there was some service going on. He turned and beckoned me in with a smile, so I thought he had found it was just someone practising. To my amazement the church was empty and silent. We sat down near the organ for a moment and he said, 'Have you heard the story of the organ playing before?' I assured him I had not. Nothing was farther from my mind at the time. All I thought of was that I hoped we would hear the footsteps. We afterwards went up and down the path several times to see if we could hear it again but could not. The whole event was over in half a minute, and it was absolutely impossible for anyone to have escaped in the time. We went all over the church. From the time when I stopped to the time Mr Henning rushed into the church was a matter of seconds. No one could possibly have been there and got away in the time. Besides, how could they know we were coming? From the outside it sounded just like church music, without voices—just an organ playing as it might while the collection is being taken or waiting for a bride. Quietly, not loudly, but definitely an organ. Of course had I known at the time what it was, I should first have stopped to listen more carefully, and then I should have felt the organ to see if it was still humming. I did not think of this till too late. When I got home I found from Mr Price's second book that one other man at least had heard church music there. Also Mr Henning tells me that others have heard it. He himself has been up and down the path hundreds of times in the last ten years and has never heard it before.

In a letter dated 21 September 1950 Mr E. Woodward Jephcott of Whernalls, Alcester, Warwickshire, mentioned the similarity of this music to the sounds of a stringed band claimed to have been heard by Miss Eleanor F. Jourdain on her second visit to Versailles in January 1902. In *An Adventure* (1911) she described the sounds as soft and intermittent and was able afterwards to write down about twelve bars which were generally similar to passages in Sacchini's *Dardanus*. No one has yet succeeded in recapturing the Borley organ music so that it could be studied and, perhaps, identified.

Mr James Turner, in a letter dated 1 November 1947, remarked that in his view the organ music, if genuine, was probably 'mysterious music' not actually connected with the present organ—since if it originated from the present instrument a ghostly blower would be needed as well as an organist.

When Peter Underwood interviewed him on 23 July 1948, Mr Henning mentioned the suggestion made by a number of Borley people that the organ music was probably due to wind left in the organ. The Rector had in fact made some experiments with this explanation in mind, pumping a little air into the organ and leaving it; but he found that the air escaped immediately and when he tried the keys, no sound came. He was convinced that this theory provided no answer and agreed that the music was probably independent of the actual instrument, as Mr Turner had suggested.

At this meeting Mr Henning described how, when recently teaching a little girl the catechism in the church, a 'curious incident' occurred. There was no one else in the place at the time and the Rector could see the church porch out of the corner of his eye. Suddenly he saw a shadow as of someone standing in the porch and the child also turned. He asked her whether someone had come into the church and she replied: 'I saw a shadow.' The day was very cloudy and dull, the Rector stated, with no suddenly contrasting brilliance and darkness. Although Mr Henning had then been Rector of Borley and Liston for over twelve years, he had never before seen a shadow like this. He definitely felt that there was something strange about it. Nor had it any resemblance to one cast by someone in the church.

Footsteps, music and shadowy presences were all reported by several people in and around Borley church. Mr James Turner told us he noticed a smell of incense during evensong several times. On occasions the smell was sufficiently strong to make him glance towards the vestry to see whether any preparations were being made for the use of incense. Nothing like this was happening and, in common with other churches (including Langenhoe) no explanation could ever be found. This uncommon phenomenon, by the way, does not in all cases appear to be of a psychological origin.

Miss Susanna Dudley of Stradishall Manor, near Newmarket, reported a similar smell when, on Sunday 20 February 1949, she visited Borley accompanied by three friends, Miss Audrey Sawrey-Cookson, Sub-Lt Alastair McIver, RN and Sub-Lt Jonathan Crossley, RN. They made an excursion to Borley, hoping to catch a glimpse of the famous 'Nun', but were disappointed—as so many have been before—by that elusive lady. It was chilly and, seeking shelter, they decided to cross the road and have a look at the church. Miss Dudley provided a full report of what followed:

> ... halfway up the church path we walked straight into this smell. What struck us—or what made us think it was an odd smell, was that Jonathan Crossley could not smell it at all. It was terribly strong—so strong that the rest of us had to walk over and breathe clean air—but Jonathan *could not smell it*. Yet his sense of smell was (before and after) as good as ours. I can't describe the smell really, as I have never smelt anything like it before in my life. It wasn't a 'dead' smell, wasn't an animal smell—not a flower smell. It was just fearfully sickly, very very heavy and clinging and sweet, perhaps with a touch of disinfectant—Audrey Sawrey-Cookson said it was like incense—Alastair McIver said it was the most disgusting thing he had ever smelt—and Jonathan Crossley said it was our imagination! Personally, the thought

that passed through my mind was that it smelt as I *imagine* balm
—an embalmed body—would smell! I have no foundation for
this, as I have never smelt an embalmed body—! But at the time,
a sudden thought of 'disgusting, like an embalmed body' struck
me, so if you can imagine too, an embalmed body—that sickly
sweet clinging smell, heavy and nasty—that's just what it was
like! I am sorry I can't get nearer than this, but it just is most
difficult. The others find it equally hard. Two other small odd
things—one is that the smell was in one place and one only, nowhere else either along the road or in the old Rectory grounds.
Also it seemed to be in a kind of bank, I mean you walked into
it suddenly, and out of it suddenly, no fading. The patch of it was
about three yards long; I don't know how high. The other odd
thing is that there was a fairly good wind blowing at the time,
and yet, after about ten minutes inspection of the church it was
still there when we came back—in the same place—and as strong
as ever . . . We searched the area for any possible cause for this
smell such as open or new graves, but found nothing at all. I
think the fact that it was February disproves any idea of 'flower-
ing bushes' or fertilizer—and it *wasn't* pig, as since suggested in
one of the papers!

On another visit to the Borley district, over lunch at Liston
Rectory, the Rector gave us details of three puzzling incidents
which all took place in 1949. These concerned information
that was contained in a letter dated 15 March 1950.

The first incident happened during a catechism class on 20
March 1949, a Sunday, when both Mr and Mrs Henning were
in the church. It was about 10am and Mr Henning was giving a talk on confirmation. As he spoke the words 'Christ is
here', three loud and distinct blows were heard close to the
Waldegrave monument. All the children glanced towards the
tomb and apparently everyone present heard the loud knocks.
No explanation was ever discovered.

The second incident involved the apparently paranormal
ringing of the church bell on Low Sunday, 24 April 1949.
Instead of celebrating it at Borley as usual, Mr Henning
thought that on this occasion he would have the service at

Liston; he thought it likely that there would be no one at Borley, all the communicants having attended there on Easter Day. He put a notice about this in the parish magazine but Mr and Mrs Pearson, whose cottage was near the church, just past Borley Place, failed to notice it. When he arrived for evensong at 6.30 pm, Mr Henning was very surprised to find Borley church locked as he had thought that Mrs Pearson, knowing he was not there at eight am, would have unlocked the church as usual at nine or ten. He asked her why the church was locked and she said: 'But you were there at eight o'clock, both my husband and I heard the bell!' They would hardly believe that the Rector had not been there, as they both remarked on the bell; Mrs Pearson told her husband 'It's Communion morning'. This incident may be regarded as impressive because both the Pearsons had always been sceptical about the haunting.

The third incident concerned Mr Henning's difficulty in locking the church door one day in the autumn of 1949. He and Mrs Henning left the church at about 4.30 in the afternoon. It was raining and beginning to get dark. Mr Henning was in a hurry to lock the door—but it refused to be locked. He said: 'It was just as if someone was holding the lock back.' Eventually he did manage to turn the key. Mr Henning added that in all the years he had been at Borley that key had always turned quite easily, wet or fine, so the matter could have had nothing to do with the damp. Similar incidents have been reported from Langenhoe church.

Summer seems to favour psychic phenomena at Borley. The incidents that follow all occurred during August 1949.

Early that month the Reverend Stanley C. Kipling of St Mary and St James, Barnoldswick, Lancashire, visited the place to read the lesson at the funeral of a friend. He changed in the vestry and then approached the porch to look for Mr Henning. While still inside, near the porch of the west door, he saw the figure of a veiled girl. As he looked at her, she passed behind a shrub, crossed to another close by and then vanished. He immediately went to the spot where she had disappeared but found nothing to explain the appearance or the disappearance of the lifelike and distinct figure. In a letter of 17 September 1949, Mr Kipling added that he saw the figure only for a split second and explained:

> I conceived that she was a 'frail' girl, by her stature I should say about 18 to 23. She had the shape of a nun's hood on her head from which hung the thick veiling—her features were not discernible.

It must be added that although he had known Borley for many years, Mr Kipling had previously been sceptical of the haunting. But this personal experience, for which he could find no explanation, made him seriously reconsider the whole story.

At the end of the same month, Mrs A. G. Wilson and her sister-in-law, Miss Vivienne Wilson, while on the path leading to the church heard the sound of organ music. In February 1950, writing from Dollis Hill Lane, Cricklewood, Mrs Wilson saw the significance of the experience in view of the fact that neither she nor her sister-in-law had any previous knowledge of the alleged haunting of the church.

> . . . Vivienne and I had cycled to Borley to see the Rectory, having heard that it was haunted, but having no knowledge that it had been burnt down or that the haunting extended to the church. Having discovered only the remains of the Rectory we decided to have a look at the church out of general interest. We went to the main door and found it locked, so we went by a small path to a side door. While on the path I heard the sound of an organ playing but before I could speak my thoughts, Vivienne said, 'Can you hear the organ?' We didn't give it a second thought but carried on to the side door which was also locked. Being unable to get into the church we left and at a nearby cottage purchased a copy of a booklet by the Reverend A. C. Henning (*Haunted Borley*, 1949). The first page we opened had a

photograph of the church marked with a cross at the position where the organ music had been heard, this being exactly the position where we had stood. We returned to the church but everything was silent and we confirmed that the doors were locked and there was no apparent way of getting in.

Some two weeks after the letter was written, Peter Underwood met Mr A. G. Wilson Sr of Chapel House, Long Melford, and his daughter, Vivienne, the junior Mrs Wilson's thirteen-year-old sister-in-law. From her we learned that the experience occurred about 6.30 in the evening on a Wednesday, with the weather fair and calm, without any wind. Mr Wilson added that when his daughter and daughter-in-law returned from Borley and told him of their adventure, he immediately looked up the *Radio Times* to see whether any organ music was broadcast at the time which might have been overheard from some nearby source. But there was no such programme listed on that particular day and hour.

It would appear, however, that one unexplained incident involving organ music was found to be due to the prank of two local boys who took it into their heads to play the Borley church organ—one pumped, the other handled the stops—when they heard people approaching. The boys hid among the pews and were not discovered. The visitors had heard the organ and, entering the church, found it apparently empty. So for a while this was added to the long list of 'paranormal' incidents. The boys, however, confessed to their mothers, one of whom told us about it on 2 July 1957.

On 20 August 1949, a party of four members of the now defunct Ealing Society for the Investigation of Psychic Phenomena visited Borley. After having a look at Borley church and a chat with the daughter of Mr Farrance, they started down the hill in the direction of Long Melford when they noticed two ladies standing by the garage belonging to Mr Tom Gooch. The ladies, who turned out to be Mrs Gooch and a friend, were somewhat upset because Mrs Gooch's companion claimed to have seen a figure in white or light-coloured clothing disappear behind a hedge at the back of the garage. The ladies were waiting for the figure to reappear—but it did not. Mrs Gooch told the visitors she was prepared to accept some of the reported manifestations linked to Borley. On one occasion, after she and Mrs Pearson (the churchwarden) had noticed that one of the church registers had been moved several times, they hid the book before locking the church for the night. Next morning they discovered the book had been taken from its hiding-place to a distance of some yards. The church was locked and otherwise exactly as they had left it. Mrs Gooch added that she and Mrs Pearson had also found the altar lamp inexplicably smashed on two occasions.

Later that evening, at about eleven o'clock, two of the Ealing Society's members claimed to see 'a strong white light emanating from a branch at the top of the trees on the left-hand side of the road leading to the village' at a distance of two hundred yards. The light was seen for two or three seconds only. There were no trains passing at the time nor any traffic on the road past the Rectory site.

At 12.30am a drop in temperature was recorded, followed shortly afterwards by another slight drop and later by a third and larger drop; but details are not available to establish whether these were general throughout the area, constituting the normal falling of temperature at this time of the night, or whether they were isolated and inconsistent with the prevailing temperature. Soon afterwards two members of the party thought they saw a tall, white figure take one long stride before disappearing behind a chicken house.

At 2.30 three of the visitors heard 'definite footsteps' near the road by the Rectory site; one of them thought that the footsteps sounded like 'something' or 'someone' with a limp and shortly afterwards one of the visitors, Mr Andrew M. Green, reported seeing the 'vague outline of a head, some five feet from the ground, in the hedge'.

At a meeting of the Ghost Club in January 1955 Mr S. F. C. Kiernander told us of hearing unexplained footsteps at Borley church on 7 September 1949, an evening of the full moon. Mr Kiernander had been sitting in the church porch for perhaps half an hour when he heard heavy footsteps hurriedly approaching. When he stood up, the sounds ceased instantly. He walked outside the porch but could see nothing to account for the footsteps. It was quite dark along the path leading to the church as the moon was obscured by the tall trees at the east end of the churchyard. Mr Kiernander resumed his seat in the porch and half an hour later he again heard the footsteps, exactly as before. He waited and listened and had the impression that the footsteps were approaching along the grass at the edge of the path. As they came nearer he could hear the swish of the dry grass as well as the even thud on the turf. He judged the footsteps to be no more than a yard or two from the porch. He had the sudden idea that it might be Mr Henning who knew he was at the church. Not wishing to startle the Rector in the darkness of the porch, he almost ran outside. There was immediate and complete silence. But while on the previous occasion it had been dark in the churchyard, the moon had now cleared the tree-tops and the whole churchyard and path leading to the church was bathed in the brightest light. The path was totally empty. Mr Kiernander told us he was quite certain that no one playing a practical joke could have possibly hidden in the extremely short time it had taken him to get outside the porch. He was sure that had anyone been in the churchyard, he must have seen him; to say nothing of the noise they must have made as they ran away. Next day Mr Kiernander and Mr Henning went together to the church and while Mr Kiernander resumed his position in the porch, the Rector approached the church along the grass verge on the side of the path. The effect was similar to the footsteps of the previous evening, but then they had sounded much heavier.

On another occasion Mr Kiernander visited Borley church
with a friend. They reminisced about the previous rectors.
As the name 'Harry Bull' was spoken, two distinct raps
sounded on the screen behind them. They both heard the
raps and both turned their heads at the same time to see what
had caused the sounds but there was no explanation they
could find for the isolated and distinct raps.

Two young men who lived about ten miles from Borley
became interested in the story of the haunting and visited the
place in 1949, spending some hours in the churchyard and
church porch. Their reports were dated 10 and 17 October,
drafted independently of each other. The integrity of the observers was vouched for by someone who had known both of
them for a considerable time.

They reported hearing something unseen drop in the
church porch at 9.45pm on 10 September; fifteen minutes
later they heard a creaking noise as if made by a door that
was slowly opened inside the church, followed by it slamming
and an 'unearthly rumbling noise' that lasted several seconds.
On the night of 15 October at 10.20pm while they were in
the church porch, a curious creaking noise came from inside
the church; at 11.15 this was followed by a snapping sound
from outside the porch and five minutes later something
dropped on to the roof of the porch. At 11.48pm a figure in
black was seen to walk quickly but silently towards the
priest's door and at 12.10am the sound of a key turning in
a lock was heard from the same direction. On both occasions
the correspondents remarked on the coldness they experienced in the church porch though both nights were mild:
Saturday 10 September 1949 was a night of the full moon.

One of us (PU) spent the night of 4-5 March 1950 at Borley in the company of Mr Laurence C. Gafford of Stevenage,
Hertfordshire. Several 'controls' were placed in the porch and
on the step of the priest's door. They checked these 'controls'
throughout the night and walked round the church and

churchyard but heard no unaccountable noises nor was there any alteration in the position of the 'controls'.

Seven months after this quiet night, Mr Henning reported some further knocking sounds. They were heard by his sons Richard and Stephen in addition to himself. It was on a Saturday late in August or early in September. They had gone to the church between six and seven o'clock to put things ready for the Sunday. Mr Henning went on:

> The place was deserted and very still. The three of us knelt down to say some prayers, and in the quiet came three loud knocks from about the position of the front or south door. Richard jumped up, saying, 'The ghost!' He hurried to the porch but could not see anything. I sent him along the little path towards Borley Place to see if anyone could have been working in the garden and caused the noises but no one was about. In any case I feel sure the noise was inside the church. This is the first time Richard has heard anything unusual at Borley.

It was in April 1951 that Mr and Mrs R. Bacon with their children Terrence and José and Mrs Bacon's parents, Mr and Mrs Williams, moved into the Rectory cottage. Mrs Williams died in 1959 and Mr Williams in 1972. During the years they passed at Borley (they moved away in 1972) all the family experienced curious happenings. Terrence claimed to have seen the 'Nun' three times, twice in the churchyard. On these two occasions 'she' appeared to float about two feet above ground level. (In many haunted house reports figures are said to be seen either above or below existing floor level; this is frequently explained by alterations in the position of the flooring over the years. Thus the figure is seen walking upon the floor which existed at the time of its supposed corporeal existence.) At Borley, during the course of centuries of burials, the level of the churchyard may well have risen considerably, especially as many interments took place only on the south side of the church. The corpses were formerly shrouded in wool and not enclosed in coffins; the ground was used over and over again. About 1860-80 the Victorians dealt with this problem, the churchyards were 'made respectable' and brought down to the original level. At nearby Long Melford, before such restoration, there was an accumulation of bodies round the church from two to three feet in depth. So Terry Bacon, to whom Peter Underwood talked on several occasions, may well have seen his ghost nun 'floating' at ground level as it was during her lifetime.

On Saturday 8 April 1961 Mr St John Saunders, a publisher from Chelmsford, Captain Ben Martindale from Ockenham and Mr Karl Barton, BSC, a civil engineer, spent a night at Borley. Afterwards they all reported having heard footsteps and seen bright lights for which they could not account. In a letter Mr Saunders wrote us on 11 April 1969, he described how during the all-night vigil in the churchyard, torches, car headlights and a flashlight camera all 'gave out' simultaneously. A voice was heard on the roadside opposite the Rectory site. Mr Saunders was quite sure that street lighting, reflections and similar natural explanations did not provide the answer to the pin-points of light that hovered over the Rectory garden at a height of ten to fifteen feet.

Another report, sent to us by a Suffolk JP, described the experience of a friend who visited Borley one day in 1967 with three companions in a new mini-car. They spent a little time in the lane near the church and as it grew dark saw a 'luminous white figure' in the churchyard; after a moment it seemed to change to a 'luminous white patch' that slowly moved round horizontally. They were thoroughly alarmed by this unexpected sight and so they decided to go home—but the car which until then had behaved perfectly, now refused to start and they had to push it a considerable distance before it would respond to the starter.

On Saturday 8 June 1968 a young psychical researcher, Grant Vallender, visited Borley. He went to the Rectory at

Foxearth where he met the Reverend Canon J. H. L. Pennell and they talked for about half an hour. Vallender then walked to Borley via the cart track to Brook Hall. He thought that this building was quite astonishingly like the vanished Borley Rectory. At Borley the first thing that struck him was its serenity and quiet. He spent the afternoon taking photographs and looking round. He considered himself lucky to be able to talk to Mr Arbon who had been Rectory caretaker and lived in the cottage during Price's tenancy of 1937. They discussed Borley in general; Arbon said that Price was 'a good fellow' and he remembered him well. Later in the afternoon Vallender met Mrs E. E. Payne of Borley Place who told him about her experiences, including the strange lights seen in the Rectory during the Smith incumbency. She thought Mrs Marianne Foyster was a very 'funny' woman and added she felt sure that Mrs Foyster was responsible for the 'wine-into-ink' incident that took place when Price lunched with the Foysters in 1931. Price, she said, seemed an honest man to her.

From 6pm Vallender sat in the churchyard and at about seven o'clock something he described as a 'typical poltergeist phenomenon' occurred. He was standing in the churchyard by the wall of the tithe-barn; when he looked up, he noticed a large pebble travelling over the roof. It hit the roof and fell into the churchyard. He immediately rushed round to the other side of the tithe barn but found no one there. The angle at which the pebble came over the roof showed that the throwing force behind it must have been very close to the other side of the barn. Vallender spent the rest of the night in the churchyard but nothing else of interest happened.

Mr Jon Simons of Higham Park, London, has been interested in the ghosts and folklore of Essex for a long time. He visited Borley many times without having any supernormal experiences. On 4 February 1970, a Saturday, he and Miss Marcia Matthews were reading entries in the Visitors' Book when they heard footsteps coming up the path but no one

entered the church and there was no one in the porch or anywhere in the churchyard when they looked a moment later.

Starting in April 1970, Mr G. Croom-Hollingsworth and
some friends carried out a series of extended visits to Borley,
equipped with an infra-red camera, a walkie-talkie set and
sound-recording apparatus. During a visit early in May 1970
they heard sounds they could not explain. Two gun-shots
sounded in the churchyard, three times footsteps followed
two of the party along the roadway, and on the Rectory site
they twice heard a very loud 'thud' which they believed could
not have had a normal explanation. Later they heard and
recorded on tape the sound of voices in the locked and empty
church and the sound of animated conversation, although no
actual words could be distinguished.

During a visit to Borley in June 1970 in the company of Mr
F. Connell and Mr R. Potter, Mr G. Croom-Hollingsworth
reported seeing a 'shrouded figure walking down the church
path' at twenty minutes past midnight. It was the morning of
20 June. He was alone at the time. Mr Connell and Mr Potter
were keeping watch for any appearance of the ghostly 'Nun'
from the garden of the Mills family which now occupies the
lower part of the old Nun's Walk. Mr Croom-Hollingsworth
hailed his companions by walkie-talkie. They immediately
left their vantage points and joined him in the churchyard.
He told them that the figure had disappeared behind a yew
tree. They immediately searched the locality but found
nothing to account for the figure he had seen. When they
proceeded to inspect the vicinity of the church, Mr Connell
noticed what appeared to be a light in one of the chancel
windows which moved towards the altar. Both Mr Croom-
Hollingsworth and Mr Potter saw the light and established
that the main door and the chancel door of the church were
locked and sealed.

On 18 January 1972, Mr Croom-Hollingsworth told us that
he and a party of investigators had experimented with a new

kind of sound scanner (which would pick up any sound within a radius of 500 yards) when they were at Borley in October 1970. They covered an area extending from the church door to the north wall of the church. They had no success. But in January 1972, on a night of the full moon, they repeated the experiment and picked up 'something' and tracked it on the screen.

Mr Croom-Hollingsworth synchronised a movie camera and at one time he thought he had actually obtained a moving picture of the ghost-nun. The investigators stated that they had sighted the 'Nun' previously; she appeared to be wearing clothes of a light grey colour. This time the habit seemed to be dark blue, and she followed a different and changing path.

Have all these reports been faked? Has it all been hallucination? Could it all have had a natural explanation? Quantitative evidence works in medicine or physics; it does not seem to be acceptable to many people in psychical research. Yet Borley church has yielded some secrets and may very well hold some others for the future to solve.

# 7

# *The Persistent Ghosts*

As we have seen, Borley Rectory has completely disappeared; today it is barely possible to trace the site of the former buildings. Yet curious incidents have continued to be reported ever since the rambling place was gutted by fire more than thirty years ago—not only from the Rectory site and its immediate vicinity but also from the cottage.

The cottage itself has been the centre of reported inexplicable phenomena for almost sixty years—as early as the occupancy by Mr Edward Cooper and his wife which lasted from April 1916 until March 1920.

Mr Cooper told us that when he and his wife had been in their home only six months he saw a 'Sister of Mercy' walk from the back entrance of the Rectory towards the road. This would be the autumn of 1916 when the Reverend Harry Bull was the rector. Mr Cooper and the Reverend Bull followed the figure at a distance of some six feet, but when she reached the roadway she suddenly disappeared.

An elderly inhabitant of Borley told his story to a number of people. He often used to go to the Rectory during the early evenings at this period; and when he saw a nun or 'Sister of Mercy' walking towards the Rectory on three successive occasions, he returned home, assuming that the Rector had a visitor. When he next saw the Reverend Harry Bull he commented that the Rector had been having a 'lot of company' lately and gave a description of the figure he had seen. To this the Rector replied 'Oh, that's the nun—she's always about'.

One of the servants at this period who had only been at the Rectory a very short time returned from Sudbury one evening. She told Mr E. Ambrose, the organist at Borley church at the time, that she had seen the figure of a nun standing by the garden gate. She went up to speak to her—whereupon the figure disappeared. Mr Ambrose, who related this incident to us, added that the girl was so upset by the experience that before long she left her employment.

A few weeks after the fire in February 1939 the sound of horses' hooves was heard in the lane outside the gaunt ruins.

Mr Herbert Mayes used to act as chauffeur to the late Reverend A. C. Henning. He lived about half a mile from the Rectory at Borley Green and, in the course of several years, passed the house on scores of occasions and at all times of the day and night without seeing or hearing anything unusual. That is, until 16 March 1939, when he rode his bicycle past the place at about nine o'clock in the evening. It was dark and as he mounted the hill towards the church, almost level with the Rectory gate, he suddenly heard horses' hooves coming down the road towards him.

At first he thought that some horses belonging to Mr Barnes, a farmer, must have got out of the field, and as the lane was narrow and he did not want to get knocked down in the dark by the runaways, he dismounted, stood his bicycle well back against the hedge and waited for the horses to pass. The sounds seem to come nearer and he judged that there were four horses, all at different paces. When they seemed to be almost on to him and he could still see nothing, he swung his bicycle round so that his lamp illuminated the roadway. But there was nothing to see. The sound of hooves passed him and gradually faded away down the hill. Mr Mayes recounted this experience during the broadcast 'The Haunted Rectory' which the BBC Home Service transmitted on 29 June 1947. A month before that date Peter Underwood interviewed him; he sounded convincing, and no one could shake his story.

We have mentioned the 'Psychic Fête' that Harry Price had attended on 21 June 1939, held in the old Rectory grounds to raise funds for Borley church. Soon afterwards the site and the shell of the house were bought by a Mr Woods, a contractor who levelled the ruins and sold the lower part of the former Rectory garden to Mr Tom Gooch, a Borley man. Later Captain Russell bought the Rectory site. During the successive ownerships of Mr Woods and Captain Russell practically all the bricks, timber and other remains of the house were sold. Some were used for a nearby runway on an airfield, other bricks went into the fabric of a private garage. The owner of the latter claimed that for a time curious happenings took place in the vicinity of this garage.

In 1947 Mr James Turner bought the cottage and Rectory site and four years later he sold it to Mr and Mrs R. Bacon who left in 1972 when the Priory Cottage, the Rectory site and some three acres of ground were purchased for nearly £15,000 by a gentleman called Martin.

The later period of the Borley haunting, from 1939 onwards, was dismissed by the SPR critics of the case as the 'silly season' of Borley; they saw its characteristics as 'extravagant theory, unrestrained assumption and extreme credulity'. One of the authors, however, told us in September 1954 that the Society was in fact not in a position to examine the evidence, 'having received none worthy of the name'. This being so, to dismiss the later period of the haunting seems a somewhat unfair appraisal.

We feel that the time has now come to consider some of the many, previously unpublished, reports of apparent paranormal activity around the site of the Rectory after the fire of 1939. It is, of course, for the reader to form his judgement as to the validity of the material, which we intend to record without any bias or attempt at interpretation.

Mr James Wentworth Day, the noted author and journalist, of Ingatestone, Essex, described to us a night he spent with a friend at Borley, under a full harvest moon. It was some four months after the fire. They explored the roofless dining-room and as much of the ground floor as they could. But when Wentworth Day suggested they look upstairs, he met an immediate and firm refusal from his young soldier companion who seemed convinced that there was 'something' at the top of the main stairs, watching them. Something 'huge and black', something that 'squatted, exuding evil'. Wentworth Day raised the gun he carried but his friend begged him not to shoot, feeling that a shot might start 'something unpleasant' and would probably bring local people to the spot to see what was afoot.

The two men left the ruined building and stood for some time in the bright moonlight under a tree, looking at the black, empty windows of the house. They both felt that something malevolent was watching them. Suddenly something shot between Wentworth Day's legs; he felt harsh bristles and snaky, undulating muscles. It was a gigantic black cat. It rushed into the house and it did not come out again.

A year later Wentworth Day told us that he met a London journalist who said that during a night he had spent at Borley he became convinced there was 'something very odd' about the upper regions of the ruins. As he stood outside, watching the place, a huge black cat shot like a bullet between his legs and hurtled into the house 'like a shot from a gun'. It never appeared again and when he made enquiries at the nearby farm he was told that they had no black cats, nor had anybody living around there—but that many of the people who spent a night in the garden saw a cat go into the house, always at high speed and never returning.

Three years later, in 1942, Mr Samuel Seal of Bures, an army sergeant stationed at a searchlight battery at nearby Belchamp Walter, was returning to the camp from his wife's home one dark night. Halfway up the hill towards Borley church he saw two lights coming round the corner towards him 'at the devil of a speed'. At first he thought that somebody was coasting down the hill in a car since he heard no sound; then, as the lights came nearer, they suddenly 'switched across the road' and he caught a glimpse of a dark shape following them. He decided that a car or carriage of some kind had swept into the Rectory drive, but when he arrived at the entrance, only seconds later, the gate was closed and there was no sign of any vehicle in the forecourt of the burnt-out building. At the time Mr Seal told the story to us in 1947, he had not heard about the reported haunting of Borley.

On 6 and 7 June 1944, three medical students (now qualified doctors) visited the Rectory ruins and sent a full report of their all-night vigil. At about 1.30am it began to rain, so they moved into what had been the scullery. After a few minutes they all heard the sound of steady, slow footsteps from the ceiling above, as if a tired man were walking about in heavy boots. They made a careful search but were unable to find anything to account for the sounds. There were no other visitors on the site at the time.

So the footsteps, the first recorded phenomenon in 1886 and subsequently reported by most of the occupants and many visitors, had 'survived' the fire. Unexplained footsteps continued to be heard from the Rectory site and the vicinity of the cottage, and in March 1950 Peter Underwood and a companion three times heard footsteps from the empty room above them while spending a night in the cottage.

Some people maintained that curious events resulted when they took away a relic from the old Rectory. One young man, his parents and others who were involved in such an experience all persisted in maintaining that everything happened exactly as they described it to us.

In 1946, shortly after starting his career as a journalist,

Montague Elelman of Beckenham went to Borley with the vague idea of picking up a story for a London paper. He wandered about the ruins for a little while, and when he left, he picked up a piece of a charred oak beam as a souvenir. No one knew where he had been. Late that evening he put the memento of Borley on the mantelpiece in the room he was occupying in his married sister's home in London. He was downstairs getting ready for dinner when he heard his sister cry out upstairs. She came into the dining-room, looking pale and distressed. She explained that as she passed the open door of her brother's room, she had seen what looked like 'a black-garbed nun' standing motionless in the gloom. Naturally everybody agreed that it must have been a trick of the light. Mr Elelman decided to postpone telling the story of his visit to Borley. That night he dreamed about a nun and it seemed that someone was shouting the word 'Borley!'. He saw a nun gliding up to him, her skin 'like grey leather'. She looked at him with her dead eyes and as she screamed, he woke suddenly.

Next day his brother arrived for a short visit and it was arranged that they should share the same bedroom. Elelman told him about Borley and its ghosts but his brother was sceptical. Although the weather was mild, during the night Montague Elelman's brother became troubled by intense cold; he lay in bed with chattering teeth and afterwards said that he seemed to hear a voice telling him: 'Sit up!'

The following night both brothers were awakened at 2.30 am by a loud, irregular chiming sound. They knew there were no chiming clocks in the house, yet the noise appeared to come from somewhere inside. It was never explained, nor repeated.

A few weeks later Mr Elelman moved into lodgings at Westcliff-on-Sea. He left the piece of charred wood at the cheerful little house and went to spend a weekend in Surrey. When he returned on the Monday evening, his landlord and his wife told him that on Friday and Saturday they had been disturbed by prolonged ringing of their doorbell—on both days at eight o'clock in the evening. No one was at the door when they answered. Suspecting that someone was playing a joke on them, on Sunday they closed the glass inner door but at 8 o'clock the ringing sounded again. Mr Garnett, the land-lord, hurried out but saw from the hall that no one was at the front door—yet the bell continued to shrill as he watched.

On Monday afternoon Mrs Garnett was chatting with a neighbour at the door when her companion enquired about the darkly clad figure she had just glimpsed on the stair landing behind Mrs Garnett. Mrs Garnett was alone in the house at the time. Mr Elelman maintains that during the nine years he possessed the piece of charred wood odd and inex-plicable things continued to happen around it.

At the end of April 1950 Peter Underwood received an in-teresting letter from Mr John May of Bury St Edmunds, de-tailing a curious incident that happened to him when visiting the Borley site early in May 1947. He wrote:

> I have been very successful in exorcising unquiet spirits and I have been familiar with the tales of the Borley Rectory hauntings for many years. On a hot July day in 1946 I decided to cycle over to Borley from Redgrave. I would stress the fact that it was a very hot sultry day with more than a hint of thundery storm in the air; the sky was clear, blue and cloudless. I reached the old Rec-tory gate about two o'clock when the heat of the afternoon was at its greatest. I recall that I was perspiring as I leaned my bicycle against the hedge. I stood in the shade of the tree where the nun is said to have materialized, in order to cool off a little, and noticed nothing strange; in was a typical forlorn and unkempt garden. I moved over to the right from the shade to where the sun was flecking the ground through the leaves of tall bushes. The ground was littered with dead leaves and the dead branches of the bushes. Without warning, and very suddenly, I sensed a cold wave of air. It was not the coolness of a breeze—but the sticky, damp, raw cold, that one would expect to meet on entering a deep underground tomb. So great was my awareness of this cold

that I started back to my bicycle to get my jacket. It was then that the most extraordinary phenomenon of the afternoon began. A stout stick rose seemingly unaided from the ground and waved itself about six inches from my nose. It waved backwards and forwards for several inches, then soared away in an arc and fell some distance away among the shrubs.

I thereupon said a prayer, taken from an old manuscript of exorcism which I came upon in Rome during the war:

'Oh unquiet spirit, who at thy release from the contagion of the flesh choosest to remain earthbound and haunt this spot, go thy way, rejoicing that the prayers of the faithful shall follow thee, that thou mayest enjoy everlasting rest and peace, and at the end mayest find thy rightful place at the Throne of Grace, Amen.'

Alas, whoever and whatever was active on the site of the burnt-out Rectory did not appear to respond to Mr May's prayer. Unexplained incidents continued almost unabated.

In May 1947 the Reverend A. C. Henning related the story of the curious behaviour of a water diviner's twig on the Rectory site. (He had already given some details of it in a letter dated 19 September 1946.) A water diviner was trying to find water for Mr Gooch, owner of the lower part of the old Rectory grounds. At a certain spot the stick bent over with such force that Mr Gooch could hardly force it up again in the diviner's hands. The latter was puzzled and told Mr Gooch she thought there might be treasure at that place. Mr Gooch repeated this to Mr Henning who immediately thought of the church plate, which, according to local tradition, had been buried in the grounds. The spot was carefully marked and later a good deal of excavation was carried out. Between attempts at digging, the twig was usually placed, for convenience, in a nearby tree. One morning Mr Gooch found it outside his home, some distance away. He took it back to the Rectory grounds and replaced it between the branches of the tree. Next morning he again found it near his home, only a few feet from the spot where he had previously discovered it.

No treasure or anything of interest was found during the digging operations carried out at the place indicated by the diviner. Even when several men from the BBC—who visited Borley in connection with the programme, 'The Haunted Rectory', broadcast on Sunday 29 June 1947—assisted with the digging and reached a depth of nine feet, the results were entirely negative. As a test some silver was hidden under the ploughed-up lawn, unknown to the diviner—but she immediately found it. The digging included a large hole near one of Mr Gooch's walnut trees. Soon after the hole was filled in, a violent storm hit the district and tore down the walnut tree which fell exactly where the digging had been taking place.

Dr C. C. P. Hilton-Rowe, formerly of the Bank of England, visited Borley in March 1947 to take photographs of the interior of the church. On 8 March he wrote:

I arrived at Borley at 10 a.m. last Monday and immediately made myself known to the Rev A. C. Henning, Harry Price having informed me that he would like a photograph of the Waldegrave tomb and the grave of the Rev H. D. E. Bull. At Borley I took the photographs for which Price asked, and others in addition. For the purpose of determining correct exposures I have been accustomed to use an 'Avo' Exposure Meter (photo-electric cell type). This exposure meter I used at the church. After taking the pictures I walked to the gate at which Fred Cartwright saw the Nun. I saw that the mechanism operating the main well and a small part of the brickwork surmounted by a cistern were all that remained of the Rectory. I was wondering whether it would be worth while taking an exposure and produced the meter to test the light. To my surprise the meter failed to respond, but by tapping the meter very hard I jerked the needle to another position where it was again immobile. It was not until I left the gate that the needle behaved in a normal manner. I have had no trouble with it since.

We discussed this experience, ghosts in general and Borley in particular, on many occasions with Dr Hilton-Rowe at the

Ghost Club and at his former home, the Wick Farm, Ardleigh, Colchester.

In his letter Dr Hilton-Rowe mentioned the digging up of one of the graves in the cats' cemetery, discovered by Mr Sidney H. Glanville and his son on 14 August 1937, and made the interesting suggestion that perhaps the lost plate of Borley church had been buried there and was retrieved by the person or persons who so hastily and surreptitiously disturbed the graves.

According to various planchette messages, 17 May 1947 was the 280th anniversary of the death of the elusive Marie Lairre. It was on that date that Peter Underwood first met Mr and Mrs James Turner who had then been at the cottage (known as Borley Priory) for only three weeks. During his stay at Borley, Mr Turner, a well-known poet, a successful writer and broadcaster, combined these vocations with fruit farming and mushroom-growing. He succeeded in turning the neglected site into a charming spot. (This seems to be his avocation; he wrote a delightful book called *Seven Gardens for Catherine* to prove his bent and his success.) He made a sunken garden of the gaping, rubble-filled cellars and prepared to outline the site of the vanished Rectory with a low brick wall which was already beginning to take shape.

Mr Gooch, the owner of the south-east end of the original grounds, was busy putting a roof on the building he had erected, helped by a German prisoner-of-war. He related how, the night before, at about nine o'clock he was at work high up on his roof when suddenly some large wrought-iron gates which he had put up swung wide open and part of a wall (he had built a rough stone and cement wall stretching outwards from the gates to the road) fell down, although it had been built only two weeks before. Everything was quiet, there was not a breath of wind. It was a story which he repeated in the broadcast we have mentioned.

Mr Turner told us about an incident that took place only

two days before this broadcast. Mr Peter Eton and Mr Alan Burgess from the BBC visited the Rectory site. While Mr Eton stood on a concrete slab at one side of the ruins and Mr Burgess faced him on the opposite side of the site, a number of short, sharp raps were heard which apparently came from the former cellars. Mr Eton asked the raps to stop and start again —and they did stop and continue as he asked. This occurred in broad daylight. A recording of the raps was included in the broadcast.

Inexplicable odours, pleasant and unpleasant, were among the apparently paranormal phenomena experienced by various occupants of the Rectory, and we have already described some of these. Mr and Mrs Foyster reported on occasions the smell of lavender for which they could not account. At other times the inexplicable smell of cooking pervaded the Foysters' bedroom at odd times. Mr Turner recounted that both he and his wife had periodically noticed strange smells. Once it was a scent of lavender, the origin of which he was unable to discover. It is interesting to mention that both Mr and Mrs Williams, occupants of the cottage at a later date, noticed several times a strong smell of cooking—usually around four in the morning. Mrs Williams also smelled lavender when no actual lavender was present.

Mrs Bacon, during the time she resided at the former Rectory cottage, encountered a most unpleasant odour while crossing the former lawn of the Rectory. It was so strong that she attempted to make a detour and found that she was able to do this—the smell was, in fact, localised. A very thorough search provided no clue as to its origin. Mrs Gooch, in the bungalow she and her husband occupy on the lower half of the original Rectory grounds, was awakened one night by a strong smell of incense that seemed to fill the bedroom; at the same time she became aware of some 'invisible being's presence'.

Once, while walking along the Nun's Walk, Mrs Williams

heard the noise of a dog panting, which sounded close behind her. No dog was there—nor could she ever find any reason for the sound.

We have already spoken of the excavations in Borley church during May 1947. Mr James Turner took part in them. Next day, while at breakfast, both he and his wife were startled to hear a loud noise from the upper rooms of the cottage—as if heavy furniture were being moved about. Mr Turner immediately climbed the stairs to the room, where various articles were stored, but, as he mounted, the noise stopped, and nothing had been moved—nor did they find any explanation for the rather prolonged noise.

For over a fortnight at the end of May and the beginning of June 1947, James Turner was busy clearing brambles and rubbish from the Nun's Walk, working mostly in the evenings with a sickle. Each evening as he broke through the undergrowth into the old orchard, the sound of laughter and chatter came clearly to him, though no actual words could be distinguished. The voices came from the direction of the Rectory site, and as Mr Turner laid down the sickle to listen, they always died away. Sometimes he would call his wife and, as her husband worked, clearing the old path which had been hidden for so long, she would also hear the voices. But as soon as he stopped work, the voices ceased, too. Once the sounds tantalised him so much that he dashed through the brambles to try and catch some of the words—but the voices, happy and laughing, 'fled before him'. Turner said that he never had any fear of the voices—he felt only delight. When the work was finished and the path clear, Mr Turner and his wife often went to the orchard to listen but they never heard the voices again. (As we have already mentioned, in 1970 a party of investigators led by Mr G. Croom-Hollingsworth reported similar voices.)

Not many weeks after Price's death in 1948, a planchette séance in Borley established apparent contact with an entity calling itself 'Harry Price'. He stated that the answer to the Borley mystery lay in some documents which the sitters were supposed to obtain. Unfortunately, the whereabouts of these papers was only vaguely stated, although it was thought that the undiscovered crypt of Borley church was indicated.

On the evening of 8 June 1948, a séance was held at the cottage. Those present included Mr and Mrs Turner, the Reverend John C. Dening, Mrs G. Taylor of Chelsea and Mr T. S. Frankland of Trinity College, Cambridge. Messages were received from an entity calling itself 'Harry Bull' who stated, among other things, that he would haunt Borley for '4004 years'. (The date 4004 BC was calculated by Archbishop Ussher in the eighteenth century as the date of the Creation.) This figure was spelt out very firmly in reply to a direct question about the length of the haunting. Later, when asked whose footsteps had been heard on the churchyard path by Mr Turner and others, the reply came: 'Lionel Foyster'—much to the surprise of the sitters. The 'communicator' then went on to allege foul play in connection with the death of the late Reverend L. A. Foyster. These allegations remained, quite sensibly, unexplored.

The séance had started at about 12.30am. Just before 2.30 am, Mr Frankland, who was rather sceptical of the proceedings, asked the entity claiming to be Harry Bull whether, as this was the twenty-first anniversary of his death, he intended to manifest his presence that night.

This brought the prompt and clear reply: 'Go to church now!'

The sitters decided to accept this somewhat melodramatic invitation and to go over to the church porch, waiting there to see if anything would happen. The church itself was locked. It was almost dawn by this time.

The Reverend John Dening told us that most of those present expected to hear footsteps walking up to the porch, or the organ playing. Either would have been a rather alarming ex-

perience in the circumstances—probably more so than if
something paranormal had been heard when it was not expected. The sitters stayed in the church porch for some time.
The majority of them, as they admitted later, felt rather nervous and almost certain that something was about to occur—
something shocking and eerie.

Suddenly Mrs Turner, who was sitting at the end of the
porch seat in such a position as to be the first to see anything
or anybody that might walk up the path, broke the uneasy
silence by saying in a low voice: 'I don't think we ought to
be here.' This seemed to break the spell that most of those
present felt hanging over them. Mr Frankland, who was quite
calm, agreed to return to the cottage with Mrs Turner. Two
other members of the party went back some time later while
the rest waited, fruitlessly, until dawn, when they all made
their way back to the cottage.

When Mr Frankland took Mrs Turner across the road and
back into the house, he tried to put her at ease. He said he
was by no means convinced of any objective paranormal activity during the night. He added that hocus-pocus of any
plausible kind could appear to be supernormal—once the
company had induced in its members a subjective state of
mind. They had a cup of tea and then went into the dining-
room to wait for the others to return from the church. Mr
Frankland added that during the early part of the séance
he had been watching the sitters closely during the time the
words were spelled out and he noticed that whenever the wine
glass they used had moved, the flexor tendons controlling the
index fingers of the sitters on the base of the wineglass became constricted. He believed that this indicated pressure
being put on the glass, though unconsciously. He said,
jokingly: 'You know, nothing will happen if I put my finger
on the glass . . . like this . . . ' He wanted to demonstrate his
point—whereupon the glass immediately executed three wide
circles, clearly with a motive power that was far greater than

at any time during the evening. Mr Frankland, greatly startled, asked the question: 'Why were we sent to the church?' Promptly the answer came: 'Pray.'

He then asked: 'Who is in the church now?' The letters c-h-r-i-s-t were spelled out slowly and firmly. Mr Frankland immediately ended his experiment.

He told us later he was entirely convinced that something had moved the glass on this occasion; his own finger, laid gently on it, could not possibly have had the power to propel it. He thought that since the supposed entity was a priest in his lifetime on earth, the answer to his question was an extremely proper one; no one but a clergyman would have thought of such a response. Of the dozen or so occasions, at Borley and elsewhere, in which Mr Dening had participated in such a wine-glass session, that night was the only one, he maintained, on which the glass seemed 'alive'; the only occasion on which it would have been difficult for anyone present to remain totally sceptical of the possibility of obtaining messages—however garbled and confused—by this method from some kind of discarnate entity. There was obviously nothing in the least conclusive about the séance—yet Mr Dening pointed out that all those present experienced a general sensation of something 'very unusual'.

It was, of course, the following day that the Turners heard that strange, inexplicable noise of shifting furniture coming from the upper floor of the cottage.

About a month later, in July 1948, Mrs Turner was sitting in a deck chair, a couple of yards from the foundations of the vanished Rectory. She had chosen a spot under the lime trees in the drive and had an uninterrupted, pleasant view of the entire garden and the Rectory site. It was quite impossible for anyone to have entered by the drive gate without her seeing him. While she was reading, she suddenly became aware of heavy footsteps; they approached her with growing intensity and then gradually died away. She felt certain they were a man's footsteps and they sounded as if they were walking on boards—in fact, like someone walking along a passage in the house that no longer existed. A couple of weeks later the same experience was repeated in the same place.

Mr Williams also heard distinct footsteps on open ground at the back of the cottage in broad daylight. He had a clear view of the spot at the time—and it was deserted.

In September 1948 there was the very loud sound of breaking crockery in the cottage. It came from the direction of the kitchen. Mr and Mrs Turner rushed in from the dining-room to find, to their amazement, that nothing had in fact been disturbed. The noise was so loud that two workmen busy mixing concrete in the cottage yard came to the back door to ask what had happened. (We have recorded that the sound of crashing crockery had been heard before, both in the Rectory cottage by the Coopers in 1919 and in the Rectory itself by several people, among them by Mr Mark Kerr-Pearse and the Rev A. C. Henning.) Some weeks later a loud report, just like a pistol shot, was heard while both the Turners were in the kitchen. The odd thing about this incident was the loudness of the noise and that it sounded as if it had been produced actually within the room where the Turners were standing.

Mr Laurence C. Gafford and Mr James M. Sugg visited Borley on 4 August 1949. They knew very little about the haunting and they deliberately refrained from making detailed enquiries about the place, although they did glance at the illustrations in a copy of *The End of Borley Rectory* to get some idea of how the building looked before it was demolished. They had obtained permission from Mr James Turner to spend a night at the Rectory site. Mr Gafford provided the following report:

> Arriving at Borley at 10.15 p.m. we parked the car on the Rectory drive, at the back of Mr Turner's cottage and approximately outside the Sewing Room.
>
> After conversing on general topics for about thirty minutes

with Mr and Mrs Turner, Mr James Sugg and I sat in the car. The night was warm and still and a full moon was high in an almost cloudless sky.

At about 11.15 p.m. light, brisk footsteps were heard coming down the lane outside the cottage and I remarked to J.M.S. that it was probably someone returning home from the off licence at Borley Green. At the time we heard a sound similar to that made by a bicycle freewheeling downhill. In order to see who was passing I turned sideways in my seat and lowered the car window about 2½ inches, to a position just below eye and ear level, and peered through the hedge into the lane. The window-mechanism made a loud squeaking sound which entirely drowned that of the footsteps in the lane.

We listened again, but the footsteps had ceased completely, as had the 'bicycle sound'. To us, it seemed possible that we had been listening to someone walking down the lane, wheeling a bicycle. Passing the Rectory grounds and hearing a peculiar squeaking sound, this person had no doubt leapt to his bicycle and pedalled quickly down the hill. It all seemed such a simple explanation that it did not occur to either of us to investigate further, but soon we began to wonder. Firstly, the bicycle was apparently already travelling down the lane at speed, so therefore it was not being wheeled. Secondly, why did I not see any figure passing down the lane about twelve feet away? Again, is it not likely that a person, hurriedly mounting a bicycle, would make some kind of scuffing noise and probably miss the pedals at first, even though there was a fairly bright moon? In view of these points, we felt inclined to think that there was no natural explanation to the sounds we had lately heard.

During the following week whilst reading for the first time *The End of Borley Rectory*, I learnt that similar footsteps had been heard on a previous occasion and also the sounds of a bicycle freewheeling in the lane but in that case, uphill. When investigation was made as on that occasion, the lane was found to be deserted.

It was during the summer of 1949 that the apparently spectral cat made its reappearance at Borley. During the night of 28 July (traditionally regarded as 'the Nun's day') Mrs Turner was awakened by something scratching at the bedclothes, seemingly from the floor close to the side of the bed. She was not particularly worried as she assumed that one of their cats must have somehow got into the room—though there had been no trace of one when the Turners had gone to bed. As they did not like to have animals in the bedroom at night, Mrs Turner lit a candle and got up; but a thorough search by her husband (who was by this time awake) and by herself revealed no sign of a cat, either in the room or on the landing outside. The door had definitely been closed when they retired to bed and was still shut; nor was it possible to see how a cat could have conceivably scaled the sheer face of the wall outside in order to enter by the single small window. Even if it had done so—what had become of it during the few seconds it took Mrs Turner to light a candle and get out of bed? Mrs Turner concluded that she must have imagined the original scratching sound, and with no thought of anything paranormal they decided to get into bed again—when they suddenly noticed, at the foot of the bed, a dip or hollow in the surface of the bedclothes—just as if, in fact, some animal had recently been lying there. It is important to reiterate that in the circumstances it seemed quite impossible for one of their own cats to have been in the room.

As balanced and mature people, the Turners refused to accept this as a paranormal occurrence. They felt that, in spite of all the appearances, the incident must have some normal explanation. In fact, they seem to have thought little more about the incident and the intriguing possibility of harbouring a phantom cat—until, exactly a month later, on 28 August, something rather more convincing happened and made them wonder whether they should not view their previous experience in a different light.

James and Catherine Turner were looking out of the open kitchen doorway when suddenly they saw a mysterious furry form chasing Fred, one of their own cats. Thin and miserable-looking, grey-white in colour, with a scraggy tail and quite unlike any cat known in the neighbourhood, it followed Fred under the Turners' car. Fred emerged and shot up the walnut tree for safety but of the pursuer there was no sign. Mr Turner assured us that it was most unusual for Fred, who seemed very reluctant to descend from the safety of his perch, to behave in such a cowardly fashion. A careful search in and underneath the car which stood on an open piece of ground at the back of the cottage, revealed no answer to the mystery. It seemed certain that the curious furry beast could not have run off across the open space in another direction without being noticed.

Soon after this, while in the kitchen, the Turners thought they saw what might have been the same mysterious creature glide past the open doorway. They looked out instantly into the yard but there was nothing to be seen. James Turner felt that this incident was not really conclusive, yet it added to the puzzling events.

In the autumn of 1949, however, a fresh and entirely disinterested witness came into the picture. Late in October 1949, Mr Ronald Blythe, writer and former librarian at Colchester, paid one of his frequent visits to the Turners. He had had no previous experience of paranormal phenomena and was no more than very slightly interested in alleged psychic happenings at Borley. It is true that the Turners, some weeks earlier, had told him briefly of their curious experience with what they believed might be a ghostly cat, but the incident had made no great impression on him and he had practically forgotten it. Before supper Mr Blythe went upstairs to the bathroom to wash his hands. There was unusually bright moonlight shining into the room so that the visitor did not even trouble to light a candle. (The cottage had no electric light.) As he washed, he saw a distinct feline shape sliding along, as cats do, against the bath. His first and natural reaction was to assume that he had been accompanied to the bathroom by one of the two Turner cats. A moment later it struck him that the animal did not resemble even remotely either Fred or Holly. Turning from the basin towards the bath to get a better look, he found to his surprise that he was quite alone in the room. An immediate and thorough search revealed no sign of Fred or Holly anywhere in the vicinity of the bathroom. When he was asked to describe the animal he saw, Mr Blythe's account tallied to a remarkable degree with the Turners' clear recollection of the elusive furry shape that had previously given Fred the fright of his life—Mr Blythe's 'spectre' also gave an overall impression of leanness and scragginess.

In connection with this incident, Mr John Dening who was staying with the Turners at the time but happened to be on a visit to Liston Rectory at the actual time of Mr Blythe's experience, told us about the Turners' reaction to the episode—which was typical of their whole attitude. 'I well remember the quiet, nonchalant way', Mr Dening said, 'in which Mr Turner, during breakfast the following morning, remarked casually: "Oh, by the way, I forgot to tell you, Ronnie saw the phantom cat last night", and proceeded to pass on at once to some other topic of conversation, just as if the incident were quite unimportant!' Apparently it had never even occurred to his hosts to mention the matter to Mr Dening when he had returned from Liston the night before.

It might be assumed by those versed in these matters that the strange experiences such as the Turners underwent during their time at Borley would create a state of constant uneasiness and tension. But this was very far from being the case. Like the Bulls in a previous generation, the Turners accepted their 'unseen friends' as an integral part of the place. It is clear that one of the main reasons for their leaving Borley was not the occasional strange happening—which merely added a little variety to their lives—but the constant stream of uninvited and inquisitive visitors from all over the world who continued to treat the place as a kind of Mecca of psychical research.

Nothing more was seen or heard of the ghost-cat for some months until, on the night of 5 March 1950, a final and rather frightening incident occurred. Mr Dening, on another visit to the Turners, had gone to bed at about 12.30am and at once fell soundly asleep. The Turners were also about to go upstairs to bed. Mr Turner was in the sittingroom with Fred beside him on the sofa. Mrs Turner was in the kitchen while Holly, the other cat, had just been let outside into the yard. Suddenly, to use a well-worn phrase, 'the stillness of the night was rent' by a piercing feline squeal—such as a cat emits when someone treads violently on its tail. The noise seemed very close, coming, it seemed, definitely from within the cottage itself, apparently from the direction of the landing; the Turners were positive they could not have mistaken the direction of the sound. An immediate check revealed that Holly was still outside and no other cat, except Fred, still stretched peacefully on the sofa, was on the premises.

After the Turners left Borley, there have been no further incidents involving the alleged spectral cat. Here we might recall the experience of the Coopers in the same cottage thirty years previously when they were repeatedly disturbed by the sound of mysterious, pattering footsteps. Harry Price spoke of this as the 'padding dog'; the Turners' experiences suggested that it should have been the 'padding cat'. And there was the experience of Mr James Wentworth Day some ten years before, also involving a cat. As to why the poor creature should have become involved in the haunting and whether animals survive physical death and then become earthbound as some believers have suggested—the reader's guess is as good as ours. We know that many people have felt that the afterlife would not be complete without their pets.

Borley, in any case, was very much a place for cats. The Reverend Harry Bull kept anything up to 34 of them at a time—a fact that must have accounted for the need of the cats' cemetery at the south-east end of the grounds. James and Catherine Turner looked upon theirs, Fred and Holly, as a protection against evil spirits. Elliott O'Donnell in his *Animal Ghosts* (1913) expressed his opinion that cats acted as reliable psychic barometers; in his experience they invariably showed signs of terror and uneasiness, both before and during a supernormal manifestation.

It was the Reverend A. C. Henning who first told us of a curious incident concerning Dr Abernethy, a local physician. On 26 July 1949, while on her way to visit a patient at Borley village, the doctor noticed the figure of a stooping nun close to the hedge bordering the Rectory garden as she passed along the road. At first she took the figure for a real person and then, suddenly recalling stories of the Borley 'Nun', she hastily applied the brakes and backed the car down the hill. But there was no trace of anybody at the spot where she had seen the figure.

The BBC television service broadcast a film about the Borley haunting on 31 October 1955 and one of the witnesses interviewed was the lady doctor. Dr Abernethy said that judging from the face of the nun which she saw plainly, she would put her age at about forty. The figure appeared to be quite normal in every way. Both the doctor and Mr Henning made extensive enquiries throughout the neighbourhood but were unable to find any traces of a real nun having visited Borley that day. Certainly no such person had called at the Rectory cottage or had been seen in the vicinity.

This incident, of course, resembled the experience of Fred Cartwright, the journeyman-carpenter who saw a Sister of Mercy at the drive gate of Borley Rectory four times in the autumn of 1927; when, on the last occasion, he turned back to offer help, she was nowhere in sight—just like the occasion twenty-two years later when Dr Abernethy saw her.

Some seven months later, on 4-5 March 1950, Laurence C.

Gafford and Peter Underwood spent a night in the Turners' lounge at the cottage adjoining the Rectory site. This room was below the Turners' bedroom and a doorway led into the old Rectory grounds. Electrical and other 'controls' were placed in and around the church and the whole site. The vigil began at 1am after James and Catherine Turner had retired to bed. After checking the controls periodically, the investigators moved to the lounge and sat by the fire. At 2.15 heavy footsteps and muffled voices were heard overhead—simultaneously by both of them. Mr Gafford commented that the Turners were having a disturbed night. After a further 'control' check had been made and they had gone back to the lounge, once again heavy footsteps and muttering were heard by both of them. At 4.15 this was heard again under similar circumstances. On each occasion the sounds ceased a few seconds after the two men keeping vigil first became aware of them; the duration in each case was about twenty seconds.

When Mr and Mrs Turner appeared for breakfast they assured their guests that they had slept soundly and had not woken up until just before they left their beds. When they were told that movements and the sound of muffled conversation had been heard from the direction of their room during the night, they were not surprised and pointed out that on occasion the Coopers had also reported inexplicable whisperings in the corner of that room. Mr John Dening was also spending the night at the cottage in March 1950, but he slept in a front room on the first floor overlooking the churchyard. He had been up late the previous evening and slept soundly throughout the night.

While one should not ascribe undue significance to the incidents reported above, yet the facts are exactly as they have been set out. There was certainly no motive whatsoever for the Turners to mislead the two investigators and it would have been a tiresome and aimless procedure for them to get up three times during the night just for that purpose. The sounds were real and had been heard by both Peter Under-wood and Mr Gafford. And while investigators had spent many hours of day and night at the cottage during the Tur-ners' occupancy, in all kinds of climatic conditions, no other sounds remotely resembling whispering had been heard before or have been heard since. The night following this visit the phantom cat made its last recorded appearance.

For some months the Turners had been talking of their intention of selling the Rectory site and cottage. On 1 July 1950, they moved to the Mill House, Belchamp Walter, some three miles away. Later they moved to Suffolk and then Corn-wall where they now live. Mr Turner never saw the Borley 'Nun', though he would have loved to do so. During one of our many discussions about the hauntings—this particular one took place in the sunken rose garden he had made of the Rectory site—he was asked what he would do if the phantom appeared at that moment. He said, with characteristic honesty, that he did not know; one really could not foretell one's feelings under such circumstances, whether a man would be able to control his actions—but he knew that he would like to place himself in her path and see whether she walked through him. Once, while he owned the Rectory site, James Turner gave permission to an amateur dramatic society to re-enact the supposed death of the Borley 'Nun' on the spot where, according to the persistent legend, she was said to have been bricked up alive. 'I hoped the ghost nun might put in an appearance,' Turner said, a little ruefully, 'and glide behind the actress portraying her along the Nun's Walk—but no such luck!'

Mr Turner continued to visit the cottage daily from Bel-champ Walter and in August 1950 a new discovery was made at Borley. It was described by James Turner in a letter dated 24 August 1950:

... This morning while walking from the cottage at Borley into the garden, passing the dahlia bed and along the path across the old Bull orchard, which is bounded on one side by the brickwork of the stables, I noticed for the first time a break in the brickwork. It looked as if someone in the past had cut a hole there and filled it in with cement. On going closer (to see why anyone would want to make a hole at eye level) I discovered that what I had taken for cement was, in fact, a carved stone face built into the wall at the time of building the shed. The face is clearly defined though very old. The odd thing, to me, is that for three years or more I have been up and down the path and never noticed it. I am going to dig beneath it to see if it marks the spot of anything. It is a double brick wall and I hope to remove a brick on the other side and see if there is anything behind it.

It was certainly most interesting. Many times on visits to Borley and especially on the May 1947 visit when most of one night was spent a few yards from the spot, we must have passed close to the 'Face-in-the-Wall'. Until 1950 there was quite an appreciable amount of ivy covering parts of the wall of the shed and the luxuriant growth probably covered this curiosity for many years. Mr Turner did, in fact, dig into the ground below the 'Face' and explored the cavity behind it but discovered nothing unusual.

On 10 September 1950, we received from Ronnie Blythe a sketch of the 'Face'. The accompanying letter by James Turner said: 'Digging has revealed what looks like earlier foundations but it is as yet a little early to be sure. What looks like a flint wall has come to light.'

Visiting Borley on Sunday 24 September 1950, in the company of the Reverend John C. Dening, Mr T. S. Frankland, and Mr Peter Heywood of Stoneleigh, Ewell, Surrey, Peter Underwood was able to examine the 'Face' closely. He also met Mr Blythe and was able to congratulate him on an excellent drawing. The 'Face' appeared to be medieval and was seven-and-a-half inches across at its widest part, five-and-three-quarter inches high and six feet from ground level.

Digging into the ground directly beneath the 'Face', Mr

Turner came to a layer of flint at a depth of twelve inches, then one foot nine inches lower to a second and bottom layer. There appeared to be distinct traces of a flint and brick wall, probably remnants of a building that once occupied the site of Borley Rectory.

On a visit to Chilton Lodge on 8 July 1951, we learned that Miss Ethel Bull remembered the 'Face'. She believed that it was found lying about when the wall was being built and, probably at the suggestion of one of the children, was built into the wall. It may well, therefore, be a remnant of a building that stood originally on the Rectory site or possibly part of a former gravestone.

Mrs Jean Clark of Fobbing, Essex, an expert in transporting dogs to any part of the world, 'met' a ghost at Borley in late November 1950. Her curious experience took place when she was driving one dark and drizzly evening alone, except for Bugg, her cocker spaniel, on the Suffolk-Essex border on her way back from Bury St Edmunds. She lost her way and pulled up to look at her map by the light of the dashboard. Suddenly her dog, sitting in the back of the car, began to howl. Standing up, tense, it stared at the front passenger seat, its fur bristling. Only then did Mrs Clark notice a man sitting beside her. He was dressed in a long, old-fashioned fawn coat. She thought it strange that she had not seen or heard him enter the car but she knew that she had been deeply engrossed in the map. When he pointed forward she thought that perhaps there had been a bad accident and that her passenger was stunned with shock. She also assumed that he wanted a lift and started the car—but she had not travelled more than forty yards when the man motioned her to stop. Suddenly Mrs Clark realised that the atmosphere in the car had become very cold. As the car came to a standstill, her passenger just 'seemed to float' through the door. In the darkness she thought he must have opened the door silently while she was watching the road ahead. All the time the man was in the car, her dog did not cease howling. During the rest of the time Mrs Clark owned that particular car, Bugg would never get into it voluntarily but had to be lifted into the vehicle.

Shortly after the figure disappeared, Mrs Clark discovered that she was in the village of Borley. At the time this had no significance for her; during the years Harry Price had investigated the hauntings, she had lived in Germany and it was only some months later when she read that Borley was reputed to be haunted by other ghosts besides the 'Nun' that she realised the possibility that she had given a lift to one. Mrs Clark told us that she still has an open mind on the subject of ghosts but she would never laugh off ghost stories at Borley after her own experience.

In April 1951 the Rectory site changed hands again. The cottage was now occupied by Mr and Mrs R. Bacon, their two children, Terrence and José, and Mrs Bacon's parents, Mr and Mrs Williams. Mr Williams was a retired engineer, quiet-spoken, matter-of-fact and unemotional. The Bacons had plans to raise livestock and when Peter Underwood visited them on 8 July 1951, there were already some white Leghorns strutting nonchalantly along the Nun's Walk. These new occupants of the Rectory cottage began to experience a number of inexplicable incidents that included curious smells, mysterious footsteps, strange lights and the sound of a panting dog on the Nun's Walk. Once footsteps followed Mr Williams across the courtyard at the back of the house. More than once he woke in the night to find a light (a 'glow' he called it) hovering in his bedroom.

Terrence, as we have seen, claimed to have glimpsed the figure of a nun on several occasions. He told Beverly Nichols, the writer, that he saw the nun-like form disappear at a gap in the hedge. He 'thought it funny she didn't tear her dress on the brambles!' On another occasion he saw her gliding along a path near the Rectory site.

Mrs Bacon told a curious story of a tall stem of stiff, brittle hog-weed bending slowly over until it touched the ground one calm evening—and then straightening up again without any visible cause. In August 1953 Mr Williams reported seeing in bright daylight the dark figure of a nun with bowed head on the Nun's Walk as he looked out from the window of one of the former mushroom sheds. It moved or glided across the range of his vision and disappeared from view. He rushed out of the shed to intercept the life-like intruder—but there was no sign of what he had seen and the Nun's Walk was deserted. He also told us of being awakened one night by a voice; another night he saw whirling circles of light in his room which he had never seen before and never saw again, and which he was totally unable to explain. From time to time he was awakened in the small hours to smell an overwhelming odour of bacon cooking—for which no physical cause has ever been discovered. Once he got up and went out of doors— but outside there was no trace of the bacon smell. (In the Domesday Book, by the way, Borley is called Borlea—the place of the pig!)

Brigadier C. A. L. Brownlow of Sudbury, Suffolk, told us of a number of curious incidents that came to his knowledge. He paid a visit to the Rectory site and described a fire on 3 November 1953, when a newly-built shed, containing some 1,200 young chicks, was destroyed. Mr Williams showed Brigadier Brownlow the gutted shed and pointed to the path outside—the beginning of the Nun's Walk. It was from this shed that he had seen the nun-like figure three months earlier. The figure appeared to be only a couple of yards away.

In 1972, as we explained before, Mr Williams and the Bacons left the cottage and a Mr Martin followed them as the occupant.

Towards the end of 1954 Godfrey Thurston Hopkins visited Borley together with the noted broadcaster and writer, the late Kenneth Allsop, to do research for a feature story. He took a photograph of the remaining gate-post at the north-east entrance to the site of Borley Rectory with his Rolleiflex camera. This was the gateway where Fred Cartwright and others had reported seeing a mysterious, nun-like figure over the years. When Mr Hopkins's film was developed, a curious wispy, black and cloud-like shape seemed to be hovering just inside the Rectory gateway. Mr Hopkins stated he was quite certain that nothing of the kind was visible when he took the photograph. *Picture Post*, the now vanished illustrated weekly, became interested in the photograph and sent a representative to Borley; he took another photo from precisely the same position, but this time there was nothing unusual on the print or negative. Careful research was carried out by the magazine's photographic department who established that Godfrey Hopkins's photograph was perfectly genuine, that no one had tampered with it. The two photographs were reproduced in the 1 January 1955 issue of *Picture Post*; that taken by Mr Hopkins was much enlarged and captioned: 'Is this the Borley ghost?' The magazine did not attempt to answer its own question.

On a fine Saturday evening in July 1956, Dr Peter Hilton-Rowe went to Borley with a friend to whom he was telling the story of the Borley 'Nun'. Dr Hilton-Rowe stopped his car by the gate of the Rectory garden. His friend had turned towards him while listening to the ghost story and so had his back to the Rectory site. Thus he failed to see the figure but Dr Hilton-Rowe, looking towards the gate and the Nun's Walk beyond, clearly saw a nun-like apparition with her coif flowing behind her, running past the gate with short, quick steps, towards the south-east end of the old Rectory garden. The figure, Dr Hilton-Rowe told us, wore black, and since her habit was not voluminous, he gained the impression that it was a novice. Both men emerged from the car quickly and examined the site; but there was no sign of a nun or any other human being.

Then ten years later, in July 1966, Mr Gerard Kelman of

Buckhurst Hill, Essex, paid a visit to Borley with a few friends. Early on Sunday morning (24 July) at about 5am all three witnesses heard footsteps and saw a curious figure in the vicinity of the Rectory site. Mr Kelman sent a report to us immediately afterwards. He stated:

> I was standing with my back to the gate of the site of the old Rectory looking towards the church. I thought I heard sounds of someone moving on the gravel at a distance of about 20-30 yards behind me. I turned round and could see nothing. I continued to stare in the direction of the shed and then I saw a grey-blue shape appear in the half-light. At first I could not distinguish what it was but then it seemed to move forward and take two paces to the left, after which it disappeared from view. I got the impression that it was a vaguely human shape covered from head to toe in a flowing garment, such as an old-fashioned night-dress but covering all of the body.

One of his companions was Miss Jane Conolly, and her independent account states that she and her friends stood for some considerable time outside the drive gate, without anything happening. Then they all heard the crunch of footsteps on gravel but they could see no one. It was now just before daybreak and as Miss Conolly looked across the Rectory site she thought she could make out a grey figure standing by the door of the shed. Her report continued:

> Suddenly the figure seemed to move but it did not advance in a normal way. I could make out a small head on broad shoulders but from the waist downwards the figure was blurred . . . Then it moved about a yard or so to the left and eventually disappeared near the large tree at the edge of the former site of Borley Rectory. I was not afraid in any way, only delighted to have seen this 'apparition'.

A third account of this incident came from Miss Margaret Anne Conolly:

> I was standing by the gate of the cottage looking down the gravel path at the shed. I heard footfalls on the gravel and thinking it

was the owner of the property, turned to leave. Turning back I saw a figure about halfway down the pathway but it faded into the halflight before I could distinguish who or what it was. Then I noticed a slight movement by the shed and gradually could make out the lower half of a figure standing by the shed. It seemed to fade then reappear gradually, each time getting nearer. But there was no definite movement. This happened twice then it took two steps backwards to the left and faded into or behind the tree. The only time I was aware of definite movement was when it retreated. I could only see part of the figure (from the waist down), the garments were of pale grey or blue and long, flaring slightly at the bottom.

It is characteristic that of these three witnesses one described what he saw as a 'vaguely human shape', another saw the figure more or less plainly from the waist upwards and the third witness could see only the lower part.

During 1970-2 an extended series of visits was made to Borley under the leadership of Mr G. Croom-Hollingsworth and Mr R. Potter of Harlow in Essex. Numerous investigations and experiments were conducted and the visitors included persons well-experienced in the handling of delicate scientific equipment.

Early in 1970 they succeeded in recording on tape music, voices and other sounds in the vicinity of the locked and empty church.

The investigating team travelled over two hundred miles in their search for witnesses and people connected with the successive occupants of the haunted Rectory. Many had never been approached previously and now told their stories for the first time. Some were traced as far afield as Canada and South Africa.

During the course of local research they discovered a diary kept by the eldest daughter of the Reverend H. D. E. Bull. Caroline Sarah Elizabeth was twenty-one in 1885 and her fascinating record gives a picture of the Bull family that conflicts with some previous evidence.

It is hoped eventually to publish the story of these investigations independently. Such a report would include a full account of such apparent phenomena as a sighting of the ghost nun under observation, it is claimed, for twelve minutes. Afterwards a description of her habit was verified by expert authority as monastic dress.

This remarkable experience occurred early in the morning of 20 June 1970. Mr Croom-Hollingsworth was standing in the corner of the Mills's back garden, keeping watch for the ghost nun. He had been so occupied for about ten minutes. It was 1·50am when he suddenly realised that he felt icy-cold. At the same time he saw the 'Nun'. The ghostly figure appeared first near the lower end of the Nun's Walk, crossing land that now forms part of the Mills's garden, and drifted, about a foot above ground level, towards the fence bordering the old Rectory ground which was thickly wooded with shrubs and trees. Although it appeared solid, the figure passed through the fence and disappeared across the old Rectory site in the direction of the main gate near the cottage.

Mr Croom-Hollingsworth contacted his companions, Mr R. Potter and Mr F. Connell, by portable two-way radio. They were standing on the roadway between the church and the Rectory cottage. He reported to them that he had seen what he believed was an apparition and that 'she' was headed their way. At about the same time, but before Mr Croom-Hollingsworth's message came through, Mr Potter also became suddenly aware of the fact that he felt exceedingly cold. The two men, having received their third companion's message, looked in the direction of what would be the ghost nun's path if she continued across the old Bull lawn and Rectory site.

Another call came from Mr Croom-Hollingsworth: 'She's back, moving across the lawn; now she's disappeared between the bungalows.' Apparently the figure had re-appeared, re-tracing her steps across the site, and had again passed through the fence. Then she vanished for a moment between two bungalows. Her reappearance had been as quick as her vanishing; once again she seemed to glide rather than walk towards Mr Croom-Hollingsworth. She stopped about fifteen feet in front of him and he was able to study her in detail. His report states:

> Her face was one of sadness . . . the skin looked hard and dry . . . her eyes were tightly shut and she had a mole or spot on her left cheek. The coldness seemed to penetrate every bone in my body and I was becoming very scared but I couldn't help feeling pity and warmth for the very lonely figure standing in front of me . . . whatever had happened in her long ageless life-time could clearly be seen on her haggard face. She looked at least sixty . . . One could see the torment and despair of the years and one felt tenderness. I wanted to grab her wrinkled, worn hands to give some kind of warmth . . . Her clothes were grey in colour; the top half being a lighter grey; there seemed to be something like a shawl draped over her head which ended just below the bust. The rest of the dress was a darker grey and hung down over her feet.

Mr Potter and Mr Connell had been running up and down the road, waiting for the 'Nun' to appear. Now they decided to part company. Mr Connell remained on watch outside the Rectory cottage while Mr Potter went to join Mr Croom-Hollingsworth. As Mr Potter walked up the path to the Mills's bungalow and into the back garden, he noticed two figures standing at the bottom of the garden. One he recognised as Mr Croom-Hollingsworth, the other, equally motionless, was clothed in some grey material that seemed to be 'draped over her head and ended at her feet'. Mr Potter was some twenty feet from the figure and, as he stopped and watched, it turned and walked straight through the fence, crossed a ditch, and finally disappeared at a pile of rubble in the direction of the field at the back of the old Rectory grounds.

The three men supplied us with a written report; later (13

July 1972) we talked to them. It was then we learned that
the ghost nun was yet again seen near the former site of the
Rectory early in 1972.

A series of planchette séances held at Borley Rectory in
1955, 1956 and 1957, organised by Mr L. Sewell, introduced
a number of new elements into the Borley case.

The alleged communicators included Harry Price, Marie
Lairre, H. D. E. Bull, Dominic Drossy, A. C. Henning, J. O.
Steed and Henry Waldegrave. Those taking part were Mr L.
Sewell who operated the planchette and five of the occupants
of Borley Priory: Mrs Williams, Mr and Mrs Bacon, Terry
and José Bacon.

The sitters were repeatedly told to 'dig'; they were informed that the elusive church plate, including eight gold
pieces, was buried twenty feet deep under the cellars beneath
the site of the Rectory. The 'Nun', the 'entities' claimed, had
been murdered by being drowned—the murderer was a
Leslie Waldegrave who had acted on the orders of Dominic
Drossy, a Benedictine monk. Later questions elicited the information that Drossy had lived at Borley Place in 1633 and
was himself murdered 'for money' by the same Leslie Waldegrave after which he was thrown down a well at Borley.

Further direct questioning brought a rush of interesting
but frequently conflicting statements. Drossy admitted that
he had brought the Nun to Borley from Le Havre, landing at
Dover, on the instructions of Waldegrave who also paid him.
Drossy, who communicated frequently throughout the series,
particularly wanted more digging to be done at the Rectory
site. He foretold that it would bring to light 'a lot of scattered
bones' giving 'Marie Lairre' much-needed 'peace and rest'.
When he was asked about a cream jug found in a well on the
site, Drossy said it was put into the well by some of the Reverend Bull's servants; the parts of a skull that had been unearthed, he said, came from the churchyard.

Harry Price's message was 'Hurry, dig more', though he did

not say where. He went on to assert that he had never faked anything in his books. He added that 'Marie Lairre' was still at Borley and repeated his approval of the excavations that were then under way.

'Marie Lairre' asked for help to find her body. 'You must search in the cellar', she said. 'In many places . . .' which was interpretated to mean that the remains were scattered. During the last séance she said: 'I can find no rest . . . I did no sin . . . they did not believe . . . ' And her final words were simple and movingly dramatic: 'Must I walk this earth for ever?' Below this line, Mr Sewell added the note: 'Here the board went dead.'

It is very rare indeed that 'messages' from the 'other side' are clear and unequivocal. We do not know whether the ghost nun is or was Marie Lairre. We do not know whether she was murdered at Borley in circumstances as painful as has been suggested, her will and conscience outraged. Has she walked at Borley for three hundred years?

If anyone would answer these questions in the affirmative, he would also accept that nothing could be more natural than her plea to those who were trying to help her find rest and peace. In any case, can we answer the question that has been puzzling students of the Borley haunting for almost half-a-century: is this a genuine haunting?

After examining all the records and personally interviewing practically every witness, there seems to be an overwhelming belief among them and among many unbiased observers that Borley Rectory was, indeed, a centre of paranormal events. There is reasonable evidence that inexplicable happenings took place on the Rectory site and in the vicinity of Borley church, including the appearances of a nun-like figure which has been seen and described by more than a dozen independent witnesses.

Can all this evidence be exaggeration, conscious or unconcious fraud, distortion and misrepresentation? Or does the whole panorama of varied, independent and well-documented evidence establish—as far as any human testimony can establish anything—that something strange and inexplicable still goes on at places like Borley, something about which we know little and over which we have no control? The varied and frequently corroborated happenings have been witnessed by all types of people, at all times of the day and night, under all kinds of conditions.

Now and then one seems to be able to discern some sort of pattern; more usually the incidents, as so often in the world of the occult, seem to be pointless and without rhyme or reason. Perhaps they represent some kind of psychic echo or a 'photograph' etched on the atmosphere that reappears when climatic and other conditions are suitable. And there are, of course, partisans of the Spiritualist faith who believe that these are manifestations of an afterlife.

The witnesses, as we have seen, have included laymen, amateurs, the curious—but also those who are well experienced in the investigation of haunted houses. Through the long years these incidents continue to occur on and around the site of the vanished Rectory. The human bones found under the cellars have been buried by Mr Henning in Liston churchyard; fire has destroyed the Rectory and now nothing of the rambling and isolated house remains above the surface. And still these odd and apparently unconnected incidents take place. Parallels to many of them can be found in the records of the haunting in its heyday, but nothing seems to bring peace to this unquiet spot.

Varied hearsay evidence suggests that a violent and curious death occurred at Borley Rectory many years ago. Harry Price inclined to the view that there have been several tragedies, both ancient and modern, connected with the house. These need not have involved the occupiers or owners of the Rectory—but it is possible that some later tragic event, superimposed on whatever tragedy had taken place on the site of the Rectory many years ago, contributed to the already psychically receptive atmosphere which prevailed in the locality for many years. This, in turn, may have combined with the frustrations, the divided ideals, aims and religions of the occupiers at some periods—and all this may have contributed to an expectant 'electrical' atmosphere which, when invaded by an altogether different type of personality, 'exploded' with the results we have recorded. It is probable that the diverse and frequently singular personalities who lived at the Rectory or visited it all helped to produce the right conditions for the varied and spontaneous paranormal happenings.

No one has actually seen the atom; yet who can doubt its existence? To explain the vital process of photosynthesis, science had to postulate a substance named chlorophyllogen to trace the miracle of growth. These are only two examples of the beliefs which science demands, the acceptance of which are general. We are not pleading here for the Spiritualist or anti-Spiritualist doctrine but merely for the open mind; not for the suspension of disbelief but for willingness to see behind the material world forces and events that are open to different, non-materialistic interpretations.

Although there is little doubt that in the last thirty years the alleged phenomena at Borley have considerably lessened, yet they have certainly not ceased. And so the Borley story is likely to continue and provide material for yet another chronicle in the years to come.

# Appendix

# The People Who Lived at Borley

*The Bacon Family*. Mr and Mrs R. Bacon purchased the cottage, grounds and Rectory site from James Turner in 1951. They lived at the cottage (converted from the old coach house) with their children, Terrence and José, and Mrs Bacon's parents (Mr and Mrs Williams). Mrs Williams died in 1959. The entire family had curious experiences at Borley. Mr Williams and Terry claimed to have seen the ghost nun. At one time Mrs Betty Bacon, an accomplished sculptress and artist, took an interest in séances. Many were held at the Rectory cottage. She possesses one of the bells from the Rectory that are said to have rung so often without anyone touching the wires or bell-pulls. The Bacons and Mr Williams left Borley early in 1972 and moved to Great Cornard where Mr Williams died a few months later. The cottage and Rectory site were then purchased by a gentleman named Martin.

*The Bull Family*. The Reverend Henry Dawson Ellis (1833-92), MA, of Wadham College, Oxford, Curate of Holy Trinity, Ely, 1858-60, and Rector of Borley from 1862 to 1892, was a typical well-to-do squire-parson of his period. His portrait at Chilton Lodge, where his daughters settled later, showed a strong face, clean-shaven except for side-whiskers—a thoughtful and, in some ways, a hard face. He was a tall, broad-shouldered man of unusual physical strength, a keen boxer in his youth. In later years he was fond of following hounds and of potting rabbits on the Rectory lawn. He built Borley Rectory on the site of the earlier (Herringham) rectory. He and his wife were familiar with the legend of the ghostly nun and were said to have built the large summer-house in the garden for the express purpose of watching for her. The walk bordering the lawn became known as the 'Nun's Walk' during their lifetime. They had fourteen children. The last to survive were Miss Ethel Bull who died in 1961 and Miss Constance Bull who died in 1963, leaving about £50,000. The Reverend H. D. E. Bull and his wife both died at Borley Rectory and were buried in the churchyard. At his death, in the Blue Room, following his incumbency of thirty years, the Rectory had become a rambling and somewhat forbidding building, for as his family increased, a wing had been added to the isolated, red-brick, two-storeyed house on the hill.

The Reverend Henry Foyster Bull (1863-1927), known as 'Harry' Bull, succeeded his father. He had been curate at Borley for two years and before that curate at Westoe, County Durham, from 1886 to 1889. He married a widow, Ivy Brackenbury, against some opposition from his family, on 12 September 1911, in London. Mrs Harry Bull had a daughter, Constance, by her previous marriage. Constance leaned towards the Roman Catholic church. After his marriage, Harry Bull lived at Borley Place, where he had been born. His mother died in 1914. In 1920 he and his wife moved into Borley Rectory and his sisters left the Rectory. His stepdaughter Constance married at eighteen a Colonel Boothby who was considerably older than herself. He subsequently died at Cheltenham and Constance moved to South Africa where she died in 1970. (Mrs Harry Bull had died in 1955 at Hastings.)

Harry Bull would spend many hours, particularly between 10pm and 3am, in the summer-house facing the Nun's Walk.

It was said of him that he could 'hail a spectre as easily as most people can hail a friend'. Mrs Harry Bull, like the servants at that time, was not particularly interested in the ghosts and just appeared to take the haunting for granted—including the 'existence' of the 'Nun'. Harry Bull always wore an exceptionally deep clerical collar and mutton-chop whiskers, like his father's. He regularly kept twenty or thirty cats and knew them all by name; they used to follow him about, which made him look somewhat like the Pied Piper. A lovable old man, with a great sense of humour, he used to tear across to the church for matins and be back in nine-and-a-half minutes. 'Oh! very puff!' he would exclaim. 'Never missed a word and broke my own record.' He never made a secret of his numerous psychical experiences and told dozens of people of seeing the ghost-nun and hearing the phantom coach-and-horses. He had also experienced similar occurrences at his brother Felix Bull's rectory at Pentlow and other places. He died on 9 June 1927 of chronic bronchitis, in the Blue Room at Borley Rectory, like his father and mother before him. He, too, is buried in Borley churchyard.

*d'Arles, François* (real name Frank Charles Pearless). Born at Bermondsey on 10 November 1894. Married Ada Ewans, 26 December 1918, at West Hackney and lived in France for a time. Divorced by his wife, 6 November 1933. Married Jessie Irene Dorothy Mitchell at Wandsworth Registry Office, 8 August 1934. Divorced by his second wife, 11 October 1944. A month later, at Surrey North East Registry Office, married Jessie Steed (a divorced woman previously named Pring). About 1955 went to Australia where his wife is still (1972) living. Returned from Australia and, shortly afterwards, died at St Ann's Hospital, Tottenham, 10 October 1966.

Following an advertisement in *The Times* for a home for his small son, which was answered by Mrs Marianne Foyster, d'Arles boarded the boy with the Foysters at Borley and also spent some time there himself, occupying the cottage. For some eighteen months, between 1932 and 1934, he and Marianne ran a flower shop at 20 Worple Road, Wimbledon, under the name Jonquille et Cie, with Marianne returning to Borley only at weekends. For a time d'Arles lived at 128 Merton Road, Wimbledon. There is some evidence that during a certain period d'Arles dominated the Foyster household. He claimed to see an apparition at the same time as Marianne on one occasion and reported seeing shadowy figures on three occasions. Once he came down to breakfast with a black eye which he maintained had been given to him by 'a phantom'.

*The Reverend Lionel Algernon Foyster,* MA of Pembroke College, Cambridge, a cousin of the Bulls. Born in 1878. Curate of Heptonstall, 1903-5, of Oughtrington 1905-10, and Rector of Hardwick, New Brunswick, Canada, 1910-18. Missionary work in New Brunswick, 1918-27, Rector of Sackville, Nova Scotia, 1927-9. He accepted the living of Borley in 1930 and moved into the Rectory with his wife Marianne (who was twenty-one years his junior) in October of that year. A gentle and kind man who, because of his spare build and more and more crippling rheumatic afflictions, appeared to be older than he actually was. Cultured and intelligent, he was much liked in the Borley district. His wife, bright, vivacious, with bobbed hair, a 'hockey-playing type' hated the isolation of Borley and much preferred the bright lights of towns; she was disliked by many local people. She may have found life very dull there and sought and found ways of relieving her boredom.

Mr Foyster, who had stayed at the Rectory in 1895 and heard the ghost stories, believed that it was necessary to have 'psychic people' present before the 'spirits' could demonstrate. He maintained that his wife—whom he had known as a small girl when he lived near her family and visited them often—was 'very psychic' and that his predecessor, the Reverend G.

E. Smith, 'who had a lot of trouble', shared this talent. Mr Foyster always divided the Borley phenomena during his residence into two periods: October 1930 until January 1932, when, after a visit by the Marks Tey spiritualist circle, the phenomena practically ceased, and February 1932 until the Foysters left the Rectory in 1935. Mr Foyster's brother told us that the Rector sent notes round the family while these events were still going on and he compiled a book-length manuscript which he called 'Fifteen Months in a Haunted House', detailing a wealth of various psychic happenings. His brother had visited the Rectory many times and he said articles were undoubtedly displaced—phenomena for which neither Marianne nor Lionel was responsible. After five years at Borley during which the most violent, varied and vicious happenings were reported, Mr Foyster relinquished the living because of ill-health and moved to Suffolk where he died on 26 April 1945. He was the last clergyman to live at Borley Rectory. His will, dated 10 October 1922, left all 'real and personal estate and property of whatever matter and kind and wheresoever situated' to his wife Marianne who was the sole executor.

*Mrs Marianne Foyster*, wife of the Reverend L. A. Foyster. Born Emily Rebecca Shaw at 5 Guy Wood Cottages, Romiley, near Stockport, on 26 January 1899. Daughter of William Steele Shaw (described on the birth certificate as a private tutor) and Annie Elizabeth Shaw, formerly Woodyatt. Married, at fifteen, 12 November 1914 (giving her age as seventeen), Harold Gifford Greenwood, clerk, of Kensington Hotel, Belfast. Marianne's address was given as Drum-na-Dreagh, Magheramourne, near Laugharne. Her mother, Annie Shaw, and her brother, Geoffrey Shaw, acted as witnesses. She had gone through a marriage ceremony with Greenwood previously, on 8 June 1914 (giving her age as seventeen) at Stranraer, Wigtownshire, Scotland, by declaration in the presence of James Henderson McMillen (law clerk) and Maggie Isabella Glen. A child was born on 19 April 1915. Greenwood went overseas about 1920; a nephew was located in Lancashire in June 1972. No record of any divorce has been traced to show that this first marriage had ended. Marianne married Lionel Algernon Foyster at Salmonhurst, New Brunswick, on 22 August 1922, describing herself as a spinster and giving her age (correctly) as twenty-three. Marianne's young 'brother', Ian Shaw, went with the couple to Canada and Foyster paid for the boy's education.

On 23 February 1935, Marianne married, in the name of Mariane Voyster, a commercial traveller called Henry Francis Fisher, aged 34, of 38 London Road, Ipswich, at the St Pancras Roman Catholic Church, Orwell Place, Ipswich, giving her address as 12 Gippeswyk Road, Ipswich. She snipped six years off her age this time. (In a letter dated 3 July 1956, Marianne stated that she never lived at this address.) She described herself on this occasion as a spinster. She and Fisher occupied a bungalow at Woodbridge Road, Ipswich, with Lionel Foyster living, bedridden and helpless, upstairs. He was generally assumed to be her invalid father. It would appear that this was Marianne's second bigamous marriage if she had never divorced either Greenwood or the Reverend Foyster. Fisher, who died at Worcester a few years ago in an old folks' home, has a sister living near Tewkesbury and a brother who is a farmer in the Cotswolds.

Marianne's fourth marriage was to Robert Vincent O'Neil, aged twenty-nine, who described himself as 'engineer's erector, railway plant and sluice manufacturer'. Their wedding was at the Registry Office, Ipswich, on 11 August 1945, some four months after the Reverend Lionel Foyster's death. Marianne and her fourth husband gave their address as 229 Ranelagh Road, Ipswich; there is no such address. In nine years Marianne had apparently aged only two—for though she was 46 in reality, she gave her age as 32 and described herself as a widow and a high school teacher. We have no record that she had ever divorced Fisher, so this marriage, too, seems to have been a bigamous one.

The O'Neils lived at 1 Deben Avenue, Martlesham, near Woodbridge in Suffolk, where neighbours still remember them although they went to America within a week or so of the wedding. Shortly afterwards O'Neil died trying to save a child in a road accident, leaving Marianne with a baby son, Vernon O'Neil, now a member of a religious sect in America.

Marianne's child by Greenwood is still alive and is living in England. The birth certificate of this child has not been traced in Ireland, Scotland or England.

While at Borley, Marianne looked after a baby, John 'Evemond' Emery, born 25 April 1932, a child of Marjorie Emery, a spinster of no occupation, from Cobham, Kent. This child died aged five months and is buried at Borley—where inhabitants still recall d'Arles crying at the graveside. Marianne took with her to Borley Adelaide Barbara Alice Tower, born 20 March 1928, adopted by the Foysters in Canada after her mother died in childbirth and her father was killed in a farm accident twelve months later. Foyster baptised the child at Sackville on 3 March 1929. Adelaide's brothers and sisters were sent to an orphanage and have since grown up and made successful careers in Canada. In 1935, when the Foysters left Borley, Adelaide was placed in a convent where she stayed until 1940; we have been unable to obtain reliable information about her later life. Apart from the son of d'Arles, there seem to have been several other small children looked after by Marianne while she was at Borley. When she was living with Fisher at Ipswich and later at Snape, they had with them a John Fisher, born about 1936 (but not Fisher's son), and Astrid Fisher, born about 1938, who now resides in Australia.

Marianne Shaw Greenwood Foyster Fisher O'Neil now (1972) lives quietly in a small American town.

*Captain W. H. Gregson.* Purchased the Rectory in December 1938 for £500 and managed to insure the property and his effects for £10,000. He stated while the ruins were still smoking that his books were 'affected by damp' and that he had spread them out to air in the hall. A large drawing-board resting on a small chest of drawers and a two-tier medicine cabinet was used as a table to support a lighted paraffin lamp and a pile of about a hundred books. Captain Gregson noticed an odd volume among the pile by the lamp and, in extracting it, he caused the pile of books to collapse. The lamp was knocked over and in seconds the hall was ablaze. The claim on the property due to 'accidental loss by fire' was rejected by the insurance company and the matter was eventually settled out of court for £750 and costs. While he was at Borley Captain Gregson and his family claimed to have experienced a number of incidents for which he could find no adequate explanation. He lived at Walden for a while after leaving Borley.

*The Reverend Alfred Clifford Henning,* Rector of Borley with Liston, 1936-55. Ordained deacon at St German for Truro in 1911 and priest at Lincoln in 1919. He worked in eight parishes before accepting the living of Borley with Liston in 1936. He became deeply interested in the Borley story and throughout the whole of his incumbency was involved in the alleged haunting of the Rectory and, later, of the church. He and his wife and their two sons resided at Liston Rectory and took part in many of the investigations conducted at Borley by Harry Price. Mr Henning buried the human remains found at Borley in Liston churchyard. He went through many curious experiences which he was convinced had a psychic origin. He lectured and wrote on the subject, including a booklet entitled *Haunted Borley* published in 1949 and now rare. Quiet-spoken, gentle in manner and appearance, he would discuss Borley for hours on end. His wife, hospitable, much-travelled and well-educated, a person of integrity, was also convinced of the authenticity of the Borley haunting. She left the Borley area for a time after her husband's sudden death on 14 January 1955 but later returned to the district and lived there until her death some ten years later.

Mr Henning was succeeded in July 1955 by the Reverend E. L. M. Mathias. He left in 1967, moving to Gestingthorpe. Canon James Henry Leslie Pennell, residing at Foxearth Rectory and Rector of Foxearth with Pentlow from 1965, became also Curate-in-Charge of Borley with Liston from 1967 and is the present incumbent.

*'Marie Lairre'*. According to information received during a planchette séance, a young French nun from a convent at Bures who was murdered by a member of the Waldegrave family in 1667. Harry Price believed that he had established the existence of such a novice in the seventeenth century and that she did come to England from France.

*The Reverend Guy Eric Smith*, Rector of Borley, 1928-30. A Eurasian who completed his education at the University of Calcutta in 1907 and was employed in the Indian Civil Service. He and his English wife spent the early days of their marriage in India. After Mrs Smith had a serious illness, they came to England in 1924. Mr Smith studied for Holy Orders at the Chichester Theological College and was ordained in 1926. He had a curacy at Great Clacton from 1926 to 1928 when he accepted his first living at Borley, which had been offered to twelve clergymen who all refused it. The Smiths were not told that the Rectory was reputed to be haunted. A large, bespectacled man, kind, cultured and genuinely puzzled by the curious things he and his wife experienced, he informed the *Daily Mirror* which, in turn, got in touch with Harry Price. It was Harry Price's visit to Borley with a reporter that marked the beginning of an investigation lasting, on and off, for over forty years. The publicity that followed and perhaps the inadequate amenities of the large and lonely house caused Mrs Smith to become ill again. Although the Smiths had spent several hundred pounds on improving the property, there were still some bedrooms that could not be used. Appeals to the bishop were of no avail and Mr Smith looked for a living elsewhere, eventually accepting a curacy at Sheringham, Norfolk, in 1930. Having lived at the Rectory for only nine months—they ran the parish from nearby Long Melford for another nine—the Smiths left. They were usually loath to discuss the hauntings, regarding it as a subject best left alone since it was distasteful to them. Mr Smith always maintained that Borley Rectory had an evil atmosphere and that the place *was* haunted; there exist letters from him confirming this. He once said: 'Mrs Smith does not believe in ghosts.' The Smiths certainly regarded their stay at Borley as one of the darkest times in their lives. This did not prevent them from taking away a number of articles which were connected with apparently psychic happenings: the 'ticking mirror' as they called it; keys that appeared from nowhere; some of the bells that rang 'paranormally'; a 'clock that played tricks' and velvet curtains (which they bought from the Bulls) that had hung in the Rectory library for over twenty years. When they moved to Sevington Rectory the Smiths heard taps for which they could not account. After leaving Borley, they lived at nearby Long Melford for a time and Mr Smith preached his farewell sermon at Borley in April 1930. Mr Smith died at Sheringham, Norfolk, on 3 August 1940; Mrs Smith continued to live there, her memories confused and unreliable.

*James Turner.* Bought the cottage, Rectory site and land in 1947 and lived there with his wife Catherine until 1950. The Turners, who had previously lived in houses regarded as haunted, took most of the strange happenings during their stay as 'part of the furniture', like quite a few others who lived at Borley. They were never really frightened of anything during their sojourn although they experienced unexplained footsteps, bangs, crashings, voices, even a phantom cat and many other things for which they could find no rational explanation. During their time at Borley James Turner assisted with excavations in the church, dug out the old Rectory cellars, explored the wells and outlined the original Rectory area with a low brick wall. A poet and author of distinction, he wrote a satire on the Borley hauntings called *My Life With Borley Rectory,* though later he talked and wrote less flippantly about the ghosts at Borley. The Turners left because of the constant stream of uninvited and inquisitive visitors who turned up at all hours of the day and night, tramped all over the place and interrupted work with incessant questions. After living at nearby Belchamp Walter and then Grundisburgh, they settled in Cornwall where they still (1972) reside.

*Sir Edward Waldegrave* (1517?-61), politician, second son of John Waldegrave (died 1543) of Borley and his wife Lora, daughter of Sir John Rochester. A descendant of Sir Richard Waldegrave, Speaker of the House of Commons. Sir Edward, who came into possession of his estates at Borley on the death of his father, later represented successively Wiltshire (1553), Somerset (1554) and Essex (1557-8). At the time of the Reformation he was attached to the household of Princess Mary (Mary Tudor) who was imprisoned for her beliefs. As a Catholic, Sir Edward refused to enforce the order that forbade the celebration of Mass. He, too, was sent to the Tower; but during the reign of Mary he was loaded with honours. On the accession of Queen Elizabeth I he was again imprisoned and died in the Tower in 1561.

Sir Edward was buried in the Tower chapel, though some

people found it strange that his body had not been brought back to Borley. However, a monument to him and his wife was erected and this is the massive so-called Waldegrave tomb that dominates the little twelfth-century church.

One of Sir Edward's daughters, Catherine, is a 'contender' for the identity of the ghost-nun; another is the mysterious Arabella Waldegrave who may be the unnamed child on the Waldegrave monument. Still another theory suggests that a descendant of Sir Edward murdered a novice at Borley and that this act triggered off the haunting which was built up through the succeeding years by the personalities of the later occupants of the building erected on the spot where the murder was committed.

Sir Edward's wife, Frances, outlived her husband by thirty-eight years, taking for her second husband an even more fervent Roman Catholic than her first.

# Select Bibliography

Buckley, R. F. 'No Ghosts at Borley?', unpublished MS

Bull, J. M. *A Short History of Borley and Liston Churches*, 1937

Cohen, David. *Price and his Spirit Child Rosalie*, 1965

Dingwall, Eric J., Goldney, Kathleen M., and Hall, Trevor H. *The Haunting of Borley Rectory*, 1956

Foyster, Lionel. 'Fifteen Months in a Haunted House', unpublished MS

Glanville, Sidney H. 'The Locked Book of Private Information' (The Haunting of Borley Rectory), unpublished MS

Hall, Trevor H. *New Light on Old Ghosts*, 1965

Hastings, Robert J. *An Examination of the 'Borley Report'*, 1969

Henning, A. C. *Haunted Borley*, 1949

Hubbell, Walter. *The Haunted House . . . The Great Amherst Mystery*, 1879

*Inky Way Annual, Book 2*, 1948

Moberly, C. A. E., and Jourdain, E. F. *An Adventure*, 1911

O'Donnell, E. *Animal Ghosts*, 1913

Price, Harry. *Confessions of a Ghost Hunter*, 1936
*'The Most Haunted House in England'*, 1940
*Poltergeist Over England*, 1945
*The End of Borley Rectory*, 1946

Squiers, J. Granville, *Secret Hiding Places,* 1932

Tabori, Paul. *Harry Price: the Biography of a Ghost Hunter,* 1950
*My Occult Diary,* 1951

Thurston, H. J. *Ghosts and Poltergeists,* 1953

Turner, James. *Seven Gardens for Catherine,* 1968
*Sometimes into England,* 1970

Underwood, Peter. *A Gazetteer of British Ghosts,* 1971
*Into the Occult,* 1972
*A Host of Hauntings,* 1973

# Index